Investing for Retirement

Investing for Retirement

Surviving a Financial Tsunami

John Benson

11CS.03

ISBN: 978-1460966983

Printed in the United States of America

Dedication

To my wife Linda – for her patience and encouragement.

Table of Contents

Section Three: Planning for Retirement

Section Four: Investing for Retirement

Section Five: Transitioning into Retirement

Appendices

Introduction

In the aftermath of the Financial Tsunami of 2008/2009, and with losses of financial wealth exceeding 10 trillion dollars, a generation of workers approaching retirement was left to question conventional wisdom and their understanding of time honored approaches to saving and *investing for retirement.* Many were pushed far out of their comfort zones. Investor confidence was shaken as financial assets, particularly retirement savings, plunged in value. Many people questioned their decision to put aside income today for future retirement spending and their ability to understand and make wise investment choices. An abundance of conflicting opinion counseled investors to get out of the stock market before all was lost, or offered hope that this was a once-in-a-generation opportunity to invest for long-term gains.

The Baby Boomer generation has been forced to deal with the consequences of their decisions for their retirement planning and lifestyle. The issues they face are numerous and often conflicting: balancing spending and savings with income, counting on Social Security to be there for them, determining retirement plan contribution levels and investment selections, managing debt, and on and on.

As surely as the sun rises in the east it has become clear to all generations—especially boomers—that we need to step up and prepare for our retirement. We need a plan that will lead us to the retirement which we desire and want to control.

The goals for this book are to present in non-technical language a structure for developing an investment plan tailored to your unique circumstances, financial situation, and temperament; to help you implement the investment plan using established and time-tested investment principles; and in the aftermath of the Financial Tsunami, to help you understand the role your emotions play as you navigate the turbulent waters of saving and investing.

Additionally, I want to help you see the need to get serious about preparing for your retirement, understand the obstacles which can hinder your retirement planning, and help you implement a straightforward plan to save and invest for retirement. I want to help you reach the retirement lifestyle you desire by helping you to understand and deal with issues such as spending and saving, investing, inflation, Social Security, and your own unique investing temperament.

I have written this book for people who do not have a financial background. Since our schools rarely teach the basics of finance or prepare us to save and invest our money, most people are not aware they may not be financially healthy. We don't see any potential financial problem while we are young and earning more each year than we've ever earned before. Our activities are many, and our retirement plans are few; retirement is not on our radar. But eventually most of us will understand that affording the retirement lifestyle we dream of is going to take money. And having the money to pay for that lifestyle is going to take some planning.

Recognizing the challenges and obstacles you face as an investor is a crucial first step to successful investing. Challenges such as balancing your spending and savings habits, providing for unexpected expenses, selecting investments, and understanding your emotions, all contribute to your success or failure as an investor. Fortunately, when these issues are recognized, you can take determined action to deal with the obstacle. That is another goal I have for you: learning how to set yourself up for success instead of failure.

The greatest challenge you will face as an investor is recognizing and controlling your emotions.

Most people have no idea that their emotions play any role in their investing successes or failures. They feel confident when their monthly investment statements reflect ever increasing values, but they feel discouragement when their assets stagnate or decline in value. It's basic to human nature to want to add to your investments when the sky is blue and most investments are rising in value. The outlook is great. Why not continue to invest when the stock market is rising? It's comforting to know that our savings and investments are growing. But it's just as basic to feel fear and withdraw from investments when the value of those investments is in decline or has crashed as it did in 2008 and early 2009. Those parallel, but competing, normal human emotions are real and a part of all of us.

For a reality check on your emotions, let's take a look in the rear-view mirror. How did you feel during the recent economic downturn—the Financial Tsunami of 2008?

In the latter half of 2008, the economic underpinnings of world economies were shaken past the point of understanding of most people, including many of those responsible for reestablishing economic health. After several decades of loose oversight by Congress, administrations, regulators, and the financial industry, credit and financial markets had begun to unravel and ultimately lock up as consumer confidence plunged.

A perfect storm hit the U.S. Economy in 2008, as the country slugged its way through one of the longest presidential campaigns in our history. The candidates of both major parties attacked the status quo, pointing out employment losses, plant closures, and all manner of economic distresses. They pontificated as to how only they had the insight to solve the nation's problems by cutting taxes, spending more, and fixing all inequities. The housing market had been falling for more than a year in many areas of the country as real estate prices returned from the stratosphere, contributing to consumer distress as homeowners watched their home values decline. The evening news programs were filled with stories of real and potential home foreclosures, layoffs, and politicians offering comfort to the unemployed and tax cuts to everyone else, except the "rich." Many people began to wonder if they might be the next to be laid-off. And, of course, consumer confidence continued to decline from the peak reached in 2007.

This perfect storm eventually caused consumers to respond in a most natural way. As 2008 drew to a close, consumers dramatically cut their spending, further exacerbating the problem. Retail sales fell, and unemployment continued to rise as the economy spiraled downward. The stock markets responded with the biggest plunge in over 60 years as investors fled stocks for the safety of U.S. Government Treasury securities. Demand for Treasuries was so great at one point that the yield on 90-day Treasury Bills was zero; investors were willing to earn nothing in order to keep their dollars safe. A great example of how markets can go to extremes.

So how are you doing with the emotional look-back? Maybe a little uncomfortable? Are you wondering why a book about *investing for retirement* is dredging up the economic tsunami? It's because economic downturns, even tsunamis, happen. And they will happen again.

But you can prepare for downturns and recessions—even tsunamis. What's the alternative? Think about it. You need to save for retirement. You would like a lifestyle in retirement beyond the subsistence that Social Security will provide. Low yielding certificates of deposit and 90-day T-Bills will not generate the savings that you will need for a retirement of 25 or 30 years, or longer. Not to mention the impact inflation will have on those low-yielding savings over the years.

So let's deal with it. Preparing and implementing a well thought out savings and investment plan is essential.

Economic expansions and contractions (recessions) will come and go—usually many times during a lifetime—but our need to save and invest, in order to have retirement income during the years when we no longer earn wages, remains constant. And the best time-tested approach for accumulating our retirement assets is to use a combination of investments which will provide safety, stability, and growth.

The key to long-term success is having a blend of investments: stock funds, bond funds, CDs, and other federally insured investments. This is called asset allocation. As you move through your working years toward retirement, your asset allocation should adjust from higher risk to less risk and therefore provide the stability you need as your retirement approaches.

So our mutual goal is to develop a custom tailored *"investing for retirement"* plan which you can live with, in up and down economies, as you travel along the road to retirement. That is the goal that this book will help you achieve. Using easily understood, time-tested principles, and a road map designed for your unique situation and temperament, your retirement goals can be achieved.

Developing an "Investing for Retirement" plan will help you:

- See the reality of your situation and the challenges you face.
- Get serious about setting goals.
- Understand the role of your emotions.
- See mistakes to avoid.
- See your cash flow and what's available for saving and investing.
- Prepare a personal balance sheet.
- Determine your risk tolerance and investing temperament.
- Understand and select your Asset Allocation.
- Select mutual funds and ETFs for your Asset Allocation.
- Utilize pre-selected investments if appropriate.
- Implement your savings and investment plan.
- Maintain your plan.
- Prepare to enter retirement.
- Understand Social Security's purposes.
- Understand Medicare basics and how it will affect you.
- Manage and rebalance your investments.
- Establish a withdrawal plan for retirement income.
- Understand the uses and abuses of annuities.
- Gain an understanding of investing principles at the level you desire.

I have included information that addresses our different temperaments and comfort zones. Some readers will want just the basics: a straightforward plan and recommendations. Others will want to get into more detail for selecting investments and investment characteristics. Both will find their approach to retirement planning in these chapters. An Appendix is included for those wanting more depth of information and definitions.

In this book, I bring together my two careers: investment professional and adult educator/ trainer. I have now retired from both of these careers. My current endeavor is to bring both of these disciplines together to help people understand and take control of their retirement planning options, using straightforward, time-tested principles for successful saving and investing. I am an investor trainer.

I hope you will find the book informative as I walk with you through the process of planning and creating your *Investing for Retirement* plan.

Note for full disclosure: when I was active in the financial services business as a stockbroker and manager of the Investment Services Department for a regional financial firm, I held securities and insurance licenses. I sold investments and insurance products for commissions. Now that I am retired, I no longer sell investments or other financial products, nor receive commissions or compensation from the sale or recommendation of investments or the investments mentioned in this book.

Chapter 1
Reality

Chapter Objectives

- Recognize the reality of emotions.
- Distinguish between the two phases of retirement: active and passive.
- Understand the impact of inflation over time.
- Learn the reality of retirement income.
- Realize the need to set goals.

The Tsunami

October 2007, the color and crispness of fall is settling in on Wall Street and the Financial District as New Yorkers and visitors scurry about in the brisk morning air. Most seem to have a bounce in their step as they begin their day with plans and activities for enjoying the cooler weather in the Big Apple. Life is good.

The stock market has just reached a new all-time high, with the Dow Jones Industrial Average (DJIA) closing above 14,000. The sidewalks in the Financial District are more crowded than usual. Everyone seems pleasant and agreeable, even as they walk around the cameras and news crews reporting on the daily records being set on Wall Street. Yes, life on Wall Street is good.

Indeed, the rest of the country and the world are also enjoying the advances in the financial markets. Investors and Wall Street traders alike are confident in their investment planning, confirmed by the ever-increasing balances reflected in their monthly investment statements. Life is good.

Occasionally there are news reports of real estate prices declining in a few areas of the country—mostly in the areas that had experienced the highest price increases in recent years.

But everyone's investment plans are on track—just look at the results. There's no need to question our commitment to the stock market or consider changes to our investment plans. Who wants to get off a train when it is providing such a smooth and profitable ride? Life is good and our 401(k)s are even better.

Credit default swaps? Aren't those something the financial nerds use? Most people choose to ignore them, content thinking, "They don't affect me."

I have to ask, "Do you remember how you were feeling as 2008 began? How were your investments doing? How about your 401(k) or IRA? Or the plans for the new HDTV, or vacation, or new wheels? How about the balance on the credit card? Were you paying it down or continuing your quest to help a consumer-driven economy?"

Is your memory of that time and those events a little fuzzy?

Let's move forward to June 2008. There are now headlines about mortgage defaults, people unable to afford their adjustable rate mortgages, and more speculation on how long before the real estate markets recover. The DJIA had settled back a little, but was bumping along at just over 13,000 points.

Fast forward to mid-September 2008. Just under the radar of most news programs, mutual funds are experiencing increased redemptions and must sell securities to cash out fleeing investors. The flow of credit to businesses is drying up as banks conserve capital to protect against the falling value of their loans. The DJIA is down 25% from its October 2007 high, closing at 10,609 points. The financial stability of established investment and banking firms such as Lehman Brothers, Washington Mutual, and AIG Insurance is collapsing, as they are closing or being taken over by stronger firms or the U.S. taxpayer. Merrill Lynch manages to sell itself to Bank of America.

September 28, 2008: the President and Congressional leaders agree on a rescue package. On September 29, the House votes down the rescue package, and the DJIA plunges 7%. Two days later on October 1, in what seemed like an eternity for the financial markets, Congress is able to put together and pass a rescue package. The presidential campaign drags on, the economy continues to deteriorate, and by October 27th the DJIA is at 8175, down 38% since the start of the year.

On October 23, 2008, Alan Greenspan testifies before The House Oversight and Government Reform Committee. The Committee is holding hearings to get to the bottom of the financial crisis, assign blame, and determine the magnitude of the price tag to fix the problem... before getting out of town and back to campaigning for re-election.

The next day the headlines herald Greenspan's testimony: a "Credit Tsunami."

In November 2008, the Presidential election ushers in a new President and Congress, as the Tsunami continues. The Big Three automakers are asking taxpayers for a bailout. They testify before Congress that they are running out of money but not out of ideas how to make money in the automobile business. They insist their business plans are not broken; they just need a little cash to get over the bad times. Congress begins to question their business plans, and the DJIA drops below 8000. By March 2009, just 6 weeks after President Obama's inauguration, the DJIA is down another 20%, breaking below the lows set in November.

Does this help bring you back to that time?

How did you handle the Tsunami? With the benefit of the passage of time and historical perspective, take a self-assessment. How did you feel during the fall of 2008 and the winter of 2009? How about today as financial markets work through the crisis? Are your emotions balanced or still in reactive mode? Did you sell out and put your money under the mattress?

An important insight I hope you will gain from this book is an understanding of the role your emotions play in your investing successes and failures.

If there is one factor more important than any other for achieving investing success, it is the *awareness* of your emotions. I don't mean turning off your emotions—that won't happen. I mean recognize when they are kicking in and take determined action to make sure your emotions don't get you off your plan. This book will show you the importance of knowing yourself and how you will react during stressful times.

Another goal for this book is to teach you how to navigate through either a Financial Tsunami or periods of clear blue skies with its unbounded optimism, so that you arrive safely at your planned financial destination. Both unrestrained optimism in an up market or panic during a market crash will put your long-term financial goals in jeopardy.

During the Great Depression, Congress passed laws to strengthen our financial and social structure and to provide oversight of financial activities which were deemed to be in the public interest. Your personal political beliefs will dictate whether or not you see these laws as helpful or burdensome, weak or too restrictive.

But regardless of our politics, temperament, or outlook, we all live in the same reality. The same government, laws, economy, and rules of mathematics apply to all of us. Whether you are a conservative, liberal, Boomer, GenX-er, twenty-something, white, African-American, Hispanic, or any other label we may use to categorize ourselves, our economic reality is the same. The law and the principles of mathematics, finance, and investing work the same for all of us. The challenges previous generations faced are the same ones we face: health, family, finances, and lifestyle choices. It will be the same for our children. The difference between our generations is that today the choices are much greater, and a safety net is, at least to some extent, in place.

We have grown up in a world where change has been constant and the pace of life has been relentless. Just when you think you have a handle on something, a new and "improved" model is released: change. During the 2008 Presidential campaign, one candidate offered "Change," the other "Real Change." By November 2010, it was time for more change. Voters had become distrustful of the recent "Change" and voted in politicians promising more "Change!"

In our world, "real-time" information and mid-course corrections are part of the everyday discourse. We have access to volumes of data no previous generation could have imagined, much less attempted to deal with.

And with the quantity of information coming our way, it's no wonder we are sometimes overwhelmed when we must make a decision. Occasionally the information may be contradictory, making it easier to hold off making a decision until we get a little more input or time to understand the issues or digest the data. We'll get around to that tomorrow and then make an informed decision. At least for now, things are moving along, in place and "protected." That is what we think… right?

We have insurance to protect against the unexpected. Insurance that will protect against the loss of health, homes, cars, and all manner of material possessions. There is even insurance to protect against the loss of our income. And as if more comfort were necessary, our government protects our financial assets (FDIC, SIPC) and provides for our "old age" and disability (OASDI; i.e., Social Security). Those are comforting thoughts, aren't they? We are protected, aren't we?

Your answers to those questions reveal your temperament, personality, and outlook on life. They may also reflect your political persuasion or age.

We have never lived in a time when we did not have old age and financial insurance. We have not experienced a time when more than one in five Americans was unemployed, and when commerce, both domestically and internationally, was in a sustained decade-long decline.

And that can be a problem for many of us. We must guard against being lulled into a false sense of security about our finances, lifestyle, and entitlements as we prepare for retirement.

Those who have set aside personal savings and investments will be able to make numerous lifestyle choices in their retirement. Those with little personal financial resources will be much more dependent on Social Security.

The Social Security Administration estimates[1] that for one-third of Social Security recipients, their Social Security benefits represent 90 to 100 percent of their total income; and for two-thirds of recipients, their Social Security benefits represent 50 to 100 percent of their total income. That is the reality for the majority of retirees.

For many people this is going to be a cold shower. Unless you want to live the lifestyle that Social Security affords, you must provide additional retirement income for yourself – from investments, savings or a pension.

"Buzz up!" That's the attention-getting insert which the Associated Press put at the front of an article sent to newspapers and news organizations on May 12, 2009, about the just released Social Security trustee report. The article stated, "Social Security and Medicare are fading even faster under the weight of the recession, heading for insolvency years sooner than previously expected."[2]

So "Buzz up!" Let's do something for ourselves. Sitting around, lumbering toward a retirement lifestyle afforded by Social Security and modest savings, is bad news.

The good news is that unless you are already retired, you can make changes today that will affect your retirement tomorrow. A goal of this book is to show you how. If you are already retired, or about to retire, you will also learn how to balance investments for safety, growth, and income during your retirement years.

When you think about it, there are really only two things you can do with your money: save/invest it or spend it. Years ago in a class I was teaching on personal finance, after having told the class about the two things you can do with money, a young man raised his hand. He said, "John, there is also a third thing I can do with my money. I can burn it." Well, for some there may be three things, but for the rest of us, presumably more rational in our decisions, there are really only two options: save or spend. While you are working, you can more easily balance those choices and make reasonable commitments to a spending and savings plan. The choice is yours.

We live in a consumer oriented world where we are continually bombarded with suggestions of what is new and desirable. Many people find it hard to defer their wants until later, when they are better able to afford the purchase. And when they purchase the item on credit, they increase its cost and defer into the future the day of true freedom—financial solvency.

We have become a nation of spenders instead of savers, spending more than we earn—an unsustainable situation. The Commerce Department reported[3] that the personal savings of Americans, as a percentage of their disposable income for December 2006, was a negative 1.2 percent. For retirees and soon-to-be retirees, this is a formula for disaster. If there was any good news from the Financial Tsunami, it was that Americans increased their savings rate dramatically in early 2009. The savings rate jumped to more than 6%, a rate not seen in several decades—since the last severe recession. As the stock markets rebounded by September 2010, the savings rate retreated to 5.3%. When the economy fully recovers, will Americans abandon their newfound desire for saving?

If your spending habits are out of line, don't give up. In Chapter 3 you will learn how to prepare a cash flow analysis and a spending plan that you can live with. A cash flow analysis can be very revealing, especially if you find yourself spending more than you earn. It will show you areas of your spending where you might make adjustments. But "you gotta get serious."

Two Phases of Retirement

When we think about retirement, we usually picture an activity that we enjoy, with endless time to spend enjoying it and on a schedule we choose. For some it may be golf, travel, or spending the days with grandchildren. Whatever it is, we dream of having more time to enjoy it. We don't give much thought to the possibility there may be another side to retirement. Is it possible we won't be able to physically engage in those activities we longed to spend endless hours enjoying?

It's my observation that there are two phases to retirement. There is the *active phase* which comes right after we take the plunge into retirement and spend the time enjoying those activities we dreamed of doing. For many people this phase can last well into their eighties or beyond.

There is also the *passive phase* of retirement, when we no longer desire or can no longer physically do all the activities that used to satisfy us. I saw this in my parents and their friends as they aged. They loved to travel and take care of their grandchildren. But as time passed, these activities became more physically challenging, less enjoyable, and the grandchildren grew up. Our parents' generation is not unique in this transition between these two phases of retirement.

With proper planning, the active phase can be all or much of what we hope it will be, and our transition into the passive phase will come slowly and undetected. How we handle the passive phase will very much depend on our temperament and outlook on life. As I watched my parents' generation move through these phases, I noticed some retirees lived with contentment and grace, while others fought it to the end. How we handle it will be a decision we will each make.

A key retirement goal is to have the finances to enjoy the active phase of retirement and not outlive our money. Rarely have I run across someone who was planning for retirement who did not give a thought to running out of money. While this concern is normal for Boomers, it would be totally out of character for Twenty-Somethings. In our twenties we don't think about retirement. There is usually too much demanding our time and money, and too little finances to have it all. In our twenties, needs and wants are still not clearly distinguishable. For Twenty-Somethings, retirement is a foreign concept that only old people—those past forty—might need to be concerned about.

Impact of Inflation

Have you heard about the "silent killer"? The medical world tells you it's high blood pressure. Some may say it's cancer. But in the realm of finances, the silent killer is inflation—the increasing cost of goods and services over time. It affects us all. The Federal Reserve has taken it on as a major nemesis—something to combat at all cost. You should find that comforting, because in retirement, inflation can be devastating. It will eat away at the purchasing power of your financial assets and your ability to afford the standard of living you currently enjoy.

The U.S. Department of Labor keeps track of the Consumer Price Index (CPI) which reflects the prices for consumer goods and services from year to year. The CPI for the year 2006 [4] increased only 2.6%, the lowest since 2003. In 2007, the CPI increased 4.1% from 2006. Seeing the increase for one year doesn't sound too bad does it? But, $100 of goods and services in August 1983 had increased to $210 by December, 2007. That's a period of twenty-four years. Does that ring a bell? Could you be living in retirement for twenty-four years? Maybe longer? "Retirement may be longer than you think. The typical 65-year-old today will live to age 83; one in four 65-year-olds will live to age 90; and one in 10 65-year-olds will live to age 95."[5]

The good news is that you may be living in retirement for twenty-four years or longer. But the bad news is that you may be living in retirement for twenty-four years or longer. Let's choose to emphasize the good news and plan for a long retirement.

A major goal for your retirement plan will be to keep up with inflation so that your standard of living does not decline

over time. This can be achieved by setting goals and developing a plan that will balance your need for income, safety, and growth. It's the growth of your assets that will keep you up with, or ahead of, inflation. It's the safety from your investment allocation that will help protect your financial resources during the fluctuations of economic cycles; e.g., the Financial Tsunami of 2008. And it's your retirement income that will give you lifestyle choices and bread on the table.

Getting Serious - Setting Goals

For Boomers the time has arrived to get serious about planning for *living* in retirement. For younger people, there will never be a better time to start than now. It's not rocket science. It is the application of financial and investing principles which have proven reliable over time. It's a defined structure which allows adjustments for your specific financial circumstances and temperament—not a one-size-fits-all plan. Putting off the decisions necessary to set your goals, your plan, and their implementation, will only work against you. The opportunity lost for financial gains cannot be recaptured. Doing nothing about your finances is also a decision.

I have known people to rush out and throw money at the stock market hoping to "make a killing" and get in on the latest hot stock or investing trend. When questioned about their approach, they usually don't see their actions as a gamble or a high-risk venture. They are "just taking advantage" of information or acting on an idea they have just heard about. Unfortunately this occurs too frequently. (See Chapter 2, Rule 1). As we age and prepare for retirement, safety of principal becomes more important than missing out on a hot stock. The reality for 50 and 60 year olds is there is less time to accumulate financial assets than there is for the Twenty- and Thirty-Somethings, and a well thought-out, structured, and prudent plan becomes essential.

Before you set up a plan you need to define and set your goals, then develop a plan to achieve those goals. Once the plan is set, proceed with the implementation of your plan (Section 4). Don't get these steps out of sequence: goals, planning, and implementation. It could be a costly mistake.

We all have goals. Some goals are very personal, like marriage, relationships, career, time with family, leisure time, savings, retirement, etc. Goals are great motivators. We will usually make the necessary changes in our habits or actions to achieve our goals. If the goal is realistic, and we can see progress towards achieving it, we are more likely to stay with the plan as we move closer to achieving the goal. But, if there is no measurable progress, we may get discouraged and give up on the goal.

When it comes to commitment, financial goals are no different than weight-loss goals—both sets of goals need to be specific and realistic.

Here are some generally accepted principles for setting goals:

- Be specific – how much do you want to save or invest; by what date; what type of retirement lifestyle or location.
- Be realistic.
- Prioritize your goals.
- Stay involved – stay committed.
- Review periodically; adjust if necessary.

- Share your goals with someone – helps you stay committed.
- Develop short-term and long-term goals.

I hope you have already set some goals for yourself beyond the financial and material side of life. If you have not, I urge you to set this book aside and think about your personal goals before going any further.

One of the most important goals for any age group is to be free of debt. As you prepare for retirement, you need to be living within your means. I don't know your specific financial circumstances, so a blanket statement about no debt is not appropriate. But debt will burden you with a load you may not be able to carry in retirement. The monthly payments and interest, which seem manageable today, can become a real challenge. The monthly interest you pay for past gratifications can quickly become a financial and emotional burden once you begin to live with fixed income. A fixed mortgage on your home is acceptable debt if it's manageable. Will you have the cash flow to maintain the payments?

In Section 2 you will develop a cash flow analysis. This analysis will reveal your current spending pattern and help you see changes that might be necessary before or in retirement. If the analysis indicates you may not be able to afford your house payment, don't panic. Retirees have options such as downsizing or moving into rental retirement communities. It's better to see this potential problem now as you plan for retirement than to be blind-sided the month after the paycheck stops.

One final thought on goals. Don't be so rigid that you can't flex as time goes by. It's OK for goals to change as we move through life and the phases of retirement. Life changes, circumstances change, and goals will change. And we will change and alter our plan to fit our reality. Remember, don't get these out of sequence: set goals, develop a plan to achieve your goals, and then structure your finances and investments to fit the plan.

Should I Retire Early?

Sometimes I am asked, "Can I retire early?" From the perspective of a financial counselor, the answer is purely mathematical. Do the analysis: balance sheet, cash flow, projections for retirement. Do you have the financial resources to retire early?

The better question would be, "Should I retire early?" If the numbers indicate you could, then it's your choice. I can't answer that one for you. Only you can decide when to retire. Can you handle retirement? Can your spouse/family handle your retirement? Have you set personal goals that will fit a retired lifestyle?

As a point of reference, the Social Security Administration says the typical retirement age of Social Security recipients is 63 years for men and 62 years for women.

I Am Retired!

While this book presents advice for people who are preparing and saving for retirement, I have also included advice for those already living in retirement. How do you structure your investments for living in retirement? This question deals with your pre-retirement/retirement status, not your age. If you are sixty years old and retired, you have many of the same financial issues as the seventy-year-old retiree.

The process for making sound investment choices is the same for retirees as it is for those still working and so are the issues each group must understand and deal with. However, the selection of specific investments that each group must make can be significantly different. I have included two pre-selected, model portfolios (Chapter 10) for retirees who don't want to go through the process of investment selection. Both portfolios emphasize a conservative approach for your savings and investments. There is a third model portfolio for individuals who are still working and saving for retirement—those who need and want more growth potential.

Retirement begins the phase in which safety of your financial assets is paramount. You no longer have the time or wages to recover from investment mistakes. You have the same economic environmental realities as the Twenty-Something: inflation will raise the price of housing and food for both of you. The key difference is that the Twenty-Something has a paycheck which presumably can rise with inflation, the retiree has income from savings and Social Security. Section 5 will take you through the steps for transitioning into retirement.

Regardless of your status—working or retired—you need balance in your retirement plan. In Section 3, you will learn the fundamentals of asset allocation and diversification—critical components for achieving the balance between safety, income, and growth.

Chapter Questions

1. Review the economic and financial events of the fall of 2008. What was your emotional reaction to those events?

2. What can be a major obstacle to investor success?

3. What impact does inflation have on our purchasing power?

4. Should you retire early? What questions should you ask yourself to help answer this question?

5. What two phases of retirement do most people usually go through?

Chapter 2
Some Basic Rules

Chapter Objectives

- Know your investing emotions.
- Realize the link between risk and reward.
- Avoid making big mistakes.
- Get serious about retirement planning.

One characteristic that both successful and unsuccessful investors share is that they both have emotions and respond to emotional stimulation. As investors, you and I are wired to be fearful when the stock market crashes and to ignore warning signs when the market soars and market indices reach new highs almost daily. But becoming a successful investor requires us to recognize when our emotions kick in and to keep them under control. *Our natural human emotions are one of the biggest impediments to becoming a successful investor.*

Much has been written, pro and con, about investor emotions, behaviors, and decisions under the academic subject called *behavioral finance.* Often this involves some academic extrapolation of ideas as to why investors behave as they do. It asks what influences investors' levels of confidence, their projection of future events based on today's events, and what are the results of such behaviors. While those insights can be helpful, this book does not go there. This is not an academic thesis on investor behavior. This book is a practical guide, a road map, to *investing for retirement* for people who are not financial professionals.

Actions do have consequences, and consequences can have both an immediate and long-lasting impact on our lives and finances. I offer four rules which I believe are basic truths that successful investors must understand. These rules are neither secrets nor insights divined from some hidden source. These rules and their potential consequences will give you insight into yourself and provide foundational principles for achieving your personal investment goals. Keep these rules in mind as you develop your *investing for retirement* plan.

Rule 1
Know Yourself

Rule 1 - Know yourself. This is the most important fundamental principle that successful investors must understand.

We are all different. God created each of us with unique physical, emotional, and mental characteristics. We can see this as we and others express our different interests and temperaments in the daily pursuits of life. Our personalities can and will differ from each other—family, friends, and adversaries. One temperament or personality is not better than another—it's just different.

When you know yourself, that is, how you will behave and react to a situation or person, you will be able to make decisions and choices based more on reason and less on emotion. Letting our emotions influence our investment decisions will lead to disaster. Sound investment decisions are based on facts, reality, and proper planning, not emotional responses.

In 1983, when I went to New York to begin my training as a stockbroker, I was expecting to be immersed in financial, investment, and economic principles, and indeed I was. What I was not expecting was a subject our instructor introduced that first day. He told us, **"Investors are influenced by two emotions—*fear and greed.*"** He explained that we make our investment decisions based on one of those two emotions. We move between either being fearful of a future event and losing our money (investments) or getting greedy and seeing an easy profit, a continued upswing, or a sure thing, something too good to pass up.

In all the years since that morning lecture, I have never seen an exception to those two motivating emotions. The successful investors whom I have studied are the ones who recognize this tendency in themselves and make willful decisions to control their investing emotions.

Most people are not aware of these emotions when they kick in. They make investment decisions which try to take advantage of, or compensate for, fear and greed, unaware that their judgment is clouded.

Fearing the future or some catastrophic event will cause you to become too risk averse and to only consider ultra safe investments. When our greed button is pushed, we usually see a sure thing—blue skies with smooth sailing or an "undiscovered opportunity" that we need to get in on before others discover it. Thoughtful analysis of the investment or how it might fit into our investment plan is not warranted. We believe we must act now.

Your fear side tells you that you must protect your assets against possible loss. When taken to the extreme, this may cause you to invest only in U. S. Government insured investments or savings.

So is that so bad? Can you lose on an insured investment or deposit?

Yes. No-risk investing can negatively impact your retirement lifestyle. One risk we all face is the future loss of the purchasing power of our money to inflation. Unless we have a multi-million dollar portfolio to consume during retirement, we must assume appropriate levels of risk now in order that our financial resources during retirement will afford us the ability to purchase ever more costly goods and services. Being too fearful or risk adverse during our working years, will limit the return on our investments and savings.

Greed can be just as destructive to our long-range investment plan. For people nearing retirement, and those who are there now, taking inappropriate risk with retirement assets is not an option; there is little or no time to recover from financial losses. (See Rule 3 below). Greed may sometimes play out as discovering a "sure thing" or getting a return on an investment that is too good to pass up. Remember the Stanford Financial collapse in 2009? Many of the investors were purchasing certificates of deposit. The enticement was that the returns were almost double the yields available on CDs from local FDIC insured banks. The CDs from Stanford were issued by an offshore bank and not FDIC insured.

It has been my experience that greed in the extreme is more problematic for men than women. Maybe it's that testosterone thing. Maybe women are more security conscious and can better keep the greed emotion under control. But whatever it is, we all need to be on guard when our greed emotion kicks in.

A key principle is to recognize that your emotions swing between fear and greed, and to maintain a steady course as these emotions attempt to take control of your decisions.

It's not my intention that this book get into psychological issues, but a basic understanding of your personality and temperament will help you know how you are wired to respond to financial and economic news.

Knowing your temperament is another aspect of knowing yourself. Our different temperaments will cause us to respond to fear and greed in different ways and from different viewpoints. It was an epiphany for me the day I "discovered" my temperament. I learned someone had clinically diagnosed my innermost self—how I behave and respond to people and situations most of the time.

One school of thought says there are four basic temperament types: Choleric, Melancholic, Phlegmatic, and Sanguine. Each of these types has strengths and weaknesses. To find out which you are—and you may have some overlap—do a web search on one of these temperament types. The better sites will present both the strengths and weaknesses of each temperament. I suggest you concentrate on the positives, or strengths, of the temperaments until you find the one that fits you best. Then, look at the weaknesses of that temperament.

Why is understanding this important? Because it will give you an advantage in knowing how you will respond to different situations that life brings your way. For example, if you are a Melancholic, you will more likely find that some news or event will get you down more than it does other people. If the future is unclear, you will be influenced to see the possibility of downturns, disruptions, and financial uncertainty. You may think that you had better head for the hills or at least put all your assets into U. S. Government Bonds.

However, if you are a Sanguine, you may be more likely to get taken advantage of. Sanguines are very sociable and trusting of others.

When you know yourself, you will know how you will react to news and events. You will better understand why you feel as you do about your investments and your outlook for the future.

Some years ago, during a class I was teaching on investing fundamentals, I asked the students to get ready to take notes. I said that I would start the class by telling them how to make money in the stock market. I looked out over the class and noticed that everyone was looking forward, intently, with pen in hand. As I spoke, the students began taking down every word. Then I told them the secret: "Buy low and sell high." At that point a few looked up, smiling, while some continued to take notes. Eventually, as I paused, everyone looked up; they realized my obvious understatement. I'm sure some were thinking, "Come on, I paid the school money to hear the obvious. Give me a break!"

Yes, the only way to make money in the stock market, or any market for that matter, is to sell your investment at a higher price than you paid for it.

As simplistic as that sounds, it is the most challenging fundamental behavior for investors. And when we make investment decisions based on our emotions instead of sound principles, we cannot be successful investors. Selling our investments at or near the bottom of a market cycle, when things look the gloomiest, is a certainty to generate losses.

A word of encouragement at this point might be helpful. This book is not about knowing when to buy and sell stocks. On the contrary, in the following chapters you will learn how to achieve your goals with proper asset allocation by investing for the long-term, in mutual funds, exchange-traded funds (ETFs) and other investments which are appropriate for your goals and temperament.

So why is it so hard to buy low and sell high? Because we get in the way. Our emotions take over when the stock market or economic cycle goes too far in one direction. We get fearful or greedy as the market swings towards extremes. After all, who was eager to buy stocks in early 2009 as the DJIA sank to a 12-year low?

In 1999, when the "Dot Com" companies were the rage, it was so easy to throw money into a technology stock or mutual fund and watch it climb. We were all investment geniuses. What insight we had! The business and news programs were constantly talking about the "new economic paradigm shift." The old economy was so 1998. I remember one commentator saying how Warren Buffett was past his prime, his style of investing had had its day. It is true, in 1999, Mr. Buffett's company, Berkshire Hathaway, increased the per-share book value by only 0.5%—yes, a half of one percent. That did not even keep up with inflation that year.

Then came March 2000! The Dot Coms became "Dot Bombs." The markets began a dramatic and sustained three year fall. Many investors asked, "How could this happen?" What about that new investing paradigm shift? Investors' emotions swung from greed (new paradigm) to fear (losing it all). In spite of all the "new economy" hoopla, there really was nothing new under the sun.

Reality, with its economic and investing principles still intact, had re-emerged.

Many of us can remember where we were and what we were doing when we heard that President Kennedy had been assassinated or when President Reagan had been shot—events that shook our emotions. But do you remember how you felt when the market began to collapse around the technology companies in March, 2000, or when the stock market crashed in the fall of 2008 and March of 2009? Were you discouraged and frightened, or did you think this was a buying opportunity?

As it turned out, the year 2000 was not a buying opportunity, and the worst was yet to come. But neither was it the end of our economy or financial system. With a well thought out investment plan, you could have ridden out the market slump, continued to invest in a broadly diversified mix of equities and bonds—using mutual funds or ETFs—and by 2003 seen some significant gains in your investment portfolio.

During the 36 months or so that I have been writing this book, the stock market and economy have gone through significant gyrations. In October 2007, the DJIA hit an all time high. By mid-November 2008, it was down 48%. And by March of 2009, 6 weeks after the inauguration of the new President, the DJIA had dropped another 20%. Even after the stock market recovery in 2010, when Federal Reserve Chairman Ben Bernanke was asked about the direction of the economy, he said it was "unusually uncertain."

Do you remember those events? Where were you emotionally? Were your investment decisions affected? Did you panic and sell your stocks and mutual funds, or did you stick with your long-term investment plan? Did you have a long-term investment plan? Were you still in your comfort zone?

My point in bringing this up is to demonstrate that we are wired to respond to events. The stock market will continue to fluctuate, and we will continue to respond emotionally. But with a well thought out investment plan and recognizing our emotions, we can ride out these natural occurrences, stay on course, and keep moving forward toward our financial goals. The economy and stock market go through cycles. It has been that way throughout the history of commerce and will continue to be that way long after you and I have departed this world.

By the way, in his March 2009 report to shareholders, Warren Buffett reviewed the performance history of Berkshire Hathaway. From 1965 through 2008, he achieved an annual compounded gain of 20.3%. Not bad for a guy who in 1999, was so “old school.” And in the crash of 2008 and 2009, he continued to stay with his long-term approach of sound investing principles. Our emotions will rise and fall, but proven and tested investment principles will not go out of style.

Rule 2
What You Take to Vegas, Stays in Vegas

What you take to Vegas, stays in Vegas. Simply stated, this is no time to gamble. You are either in pre-retirement accumulation mode or already in retirement-living mode. Either way you do not need to be taking unnecessary risk with your assets.

For Twenty-Somethings, risk is part of life; they have more time to recover from bad investment decisions. But boomers have less time to accumulate retirement assets and recover from investing mistakes. So unless you want to continue to work until you drop, you need to become more conservative with your investments; i.e., take less risk as you approach retirement.

Unfortunately, some retirees will take greater risk with their investments than is prudent in an effort to earn higher income or make up for past losses. This is another example demonstrating that, even with the wisdom of age, emotions can still cloud our decisions.

Did you know that during recessionary times, lottery sales usually increase? The Associated Press[6] reported that in the last six months of 2008, as the recession deepened, more than half of all states with lotteries saw an increase in lottery sales. The increase was attributed in part to financial insecurity driving people to risk more of their money than usual.

This tendency toward more risk in order to make up for financial distress or recoup losses is also present in some investors' decisions concerning their investing. Some feel if they can just hit a "big one"—lottery or new stock offering—they will make up for prior losses.

It's basic to our nature to try to find the easiest way to do something. It doesn't seem to matter whether it is moving a room full of furniture or saving for retirement; we will gravitate toward the easier route. Don't misunderstand me; there is nothing wrong with finding a simpler way to do something. But don't confuse simplicity with sound judgment. When we think there is an "easy buck to be made," we are setting ourselves up for disappointment. There are no "easy" or "get-rich-quick" schemes for building financial wealth. There are sound, time-tested approaches that have worked over the years and which still work today. Don't get drawn into schemes trying to make-up for lost time or recouping losses. Review Rule 1.

Investing for retirement is not a sporting event where you give it all you've got and swing for the fences hoping to hit a home run. The most successful investors apply proven investment strategies for long-term results. They understand how to balance the inherent risks of various investments with the potential return (reward) for taking those risks. In other words, they understand the risk/reward concept: the greater the potential return, the greater the risk.

The investment plan you will develop in Section 3 is designed to get you to first base, then second, third, and finally into home plate. It is not a swing-for-the-fences strategy for hitting a home run. In baseball, the players who have the most home runs usually lead in strikeouts; and when we are *investing for retirement*, strikeouts can be disastrous.

Rule 3
Avoid the Big Mistakes

Rule 3 - Avoid the Big Mistakes. Earning money is often easier than holding onto it. It's discouraging to watch as our retirement plan is put in jeopardy when the value of our retirement accounts decline in a bear market or as that "can't lose" stock tip turns out to be a dud.

But be aware that as we invest for retirement, we are going to make mistakes. It's not possible to invest over a lifetime and not make mistakes. Investors make mistakes, and you and I are no exception. But let's be sure that a mistake doesn't sink our retirement ship. This is no time for major screw-ups. Our bungee jump into retirement will sooner or later take place.

Over the years as a financial counselor, I have observed that there are almost as many mistakes to avoid as there are people who will commit them. The following is a list of the most significant mistakes that I have seen investors make:

1. The Free Lunch

Oh, that it were so. Everyone dreams of the free lunch—something for nothing. In the financial world this is usually packaged in the "no-risk" or "guaranteed" wrapper. "Get in on the ground floor before others discover this investment and it takes-off." Or a return that is too good to pass up.

Think about it, can a salesperson really afford to spend time giving you free advice on no-risk, high return, commission-free, guaranteed investment choices? You'd never fall for such an obvious scam would you? Well, you'd be surprised how many people bite at these no-risk free lunches. (Review Rule 1.)

A few years ago, a group of employees at one company, mostly between the ages of 50 and 60, were persuaded to take early retirement and get a lump sum distribution of their retirement money. According to the NASD News Release,[7] the salesman told them they could *replace their current salary income* with monthly withdrawals. Why work? Retire now with the same income. He convinced many of them to put their entire retirement sum into an "investment" which was generating as much as 18% a year. What he didn't explain adequately was that the "investment" was a variable annuity with high-risk mutual funds and costing them close to 3% a year in expenses (see item 5 below). When the markets went south in March 2000, so did the promised returns. The retirees had to start taking withdrawals of principal to keep up with the promised level of income. By the time they realized their unsustainable situation, some had lost half or more of their original investment because of a combination of unrealistic levels of withdrawal, high costs, and stock market downturn.

It's comforting to know this type of scam has been publicly exposed so it won't happen again, isn't it? Would you believe, in November 2008, several insurance companies converted themselves into banks so they would qualify for a cash infusion from the financial industry bailout funds? Seems some were in trouble because of the guaranteed promises they had made for their indexed variable annuities. Some of the sales pitches said, "Enjoy the gains of the stock market without the risk of market declines." Yes, as someone said, unless we know history, we are doomed to repeat it. See Chapter 20 for information about the appropriate uses of annuities and annuity sales abuses.

Don't think that the only people susceptible to an investment scam or falling for a free lunch are unsophisticated investors. In December 2008, Bernard Madoff was arrested for what appears to be the largest Ponzi scheme of all time. Most, if not all, of his investors were wealthy individuals or funds run for charities and institutions. One of his investors, Stephen Greenspan, emeritus professor of educational psychology at the University of Connecticut, wrote an essay[8] in which he attributed one of the reasons Madoff's investors fell for his scam was cognition, that "anyone can have a high IQ and still prove gullible." He posed the question, "How could the risks and warning signs have been ignored by so many financially knowledgeable people?" His conclusion: “They had too good a thing going to entertain the idea that it might all be about to crumble.”

2. Uncle Lou Made a Killing...

I wish I had a dollar for every time a client came in and told me about an investment his Uncle Lou had just “turned him on to.” Please, don’t confuse relatives, friends, co-workers, and coffee shop chatter with professional investment counsel.

The investing world is awash with rumors and tips. Much of it is designed to simulate the musical chairs routine: the last guy standing without a chair loses. Or the greater fool scheme: sell your dogs (stocks) to another sucker at a higher price. This will sometimes work until someone questions the fundamental value or premise of the investment; then the stock price collapses.

Be sure you know who you are getting your investment advice from. You need to stick with sound, time-tested principles; hot tips on the latest stocks or investment schemes can be disastrous.

3. The Attorney Who Is His Own Lawyer...

... has a fool for a client. If you are acting as your own investment advisor, be careful. It can be done if you have the interest to dig in and understand the fundamental principles of investing and finance. But most people don’t come to the party with an understanding of economies, markets, or investments. For most investors, trying to pick stocks will at best be extremely difficult.

A more successful approach to this dilemma is to use proven asset allocation principles with diversification. This approach to investing is accomplished by using mutual funds and exchange-traded funds (ETFs), as you'll see in Section 4. There is no reason to head off into the world of stock picking, an approach I strongly discourage. (See Rules 1 and 2.)

4. Timing the Market

It has been interesting over the years to discover how many usually rational investors believe they can predict the ups and downs of the stock market; i.e., "time the market." By some advanced knowledge, unknown to others, they feel they will be able to call the short-term direction of the market. They believe they can either get in at a market bottom or get out at the top just before the next market decline. This has never been done consistently. Even "hot-shot" money managers who are riding high for a few years, if they hang around long enough, will be humbled by the market. You can check that statement for yourself by examining the quarterly reports of your managed mutual funds for March, June, September, and December of 2008. Did your fund manager sell out in late 2007 and stay in cash into 2009? Or even sold out half the fund's securities and kept those proceeds in cash? Of course not. And you will not be able to either.

There is a Wall Street adage: "Nobody rings a bell at the top or bottom" of a market cycle. To assume you will be able to call the tops and bottoms is not realistic. Think about it. If someone could consistently predict the top and bottom, or just one of them, they could corner the assets of the financial world in short order.

In March 2009, the stock market as measured by the DJIA dropped to 6547. Two months later, after the DJIA had surged almost 25%, closing near 8500, The Wall Street Journal[9] reported that many investors were lamenting the stock sales they made in

March, which had locked them into selling low. Some investors had sold out because they could not emotionally take the losses any longer, others sold to try and save some money for anticipated expenses, such as their children's education. Regardless of the reason, the responses could not have been worse. Selling our investments when the markets have fallen significantly and our emotions are at their lowest, is certain to lock in a strategy for investing disaster—buying high and selling low.

We can be certain that financial markets will continue to fluctuate. And that the best long-term investment strategy for success as investors is consistency with our investment purchases using appropriate asset allocation with diversification, as we invest during all phases of a market cycle. Proper asset allocation will help cushion your portfolio during market cycle downturns. When one class of investments is down, another can provide stability to your portfolio. A more in-depth discussion of the advantages of asset allocation is in Chapter 7.

Sticking with your plan will take you through the market cycles and keep you from reacting to your emotions as the new highs or lows occur. The advantage you gain from steady, rational investing is one of the strongest justifications for making sure your investment plan fits your risk tolerance and temperament. If you are outside of your risk tolerance comfort zone, there is a much greater probability that you will react to your emotions instead of staying with your reasoned plan. Understanding and determining your risk tolerance will be examined in Chapter 6.

5. Who is benefitting from this investment anyway?

I know this may sound absurd, but always ask yourself, "Who

is benefitting from this investment?" Of course it's you—or it should be. Oh, if it were only so. It's sad to learn of someone who has been taken in by a smooth talking salesperson—and they are very smooth talking. If the salesperson has been in the business anytime at all, he/she will sound very professional.

So what is my point? Just this: not all financial and investment products will benefit the client. Sometimes the salesperson is the biggest beneficiary of the investment (see above, No Free Lunch).

How can that be? Fees and commissions, the expenses charged to the owner of the investment. These expenses may be charged when the investment is purchased, or annually for as long as you own the investment, or both. Expenses become especially critical as you prepare to enter retirement and structure your investments toward a more conservative income orientation. Income investments do not have the upside potential that equities offer. The expenses to buy and hold investments, especially fixed income investments, can significantly impact the real return to the investor.

Not all investment products are appropriate for you. A good example of an inappropriate investment is the Variable Annuity. Unfortunately, today many savers and retirees are being swamped with sales pitches touting the virtues of annuities. Most variable annuities come with high fees and expenses and will lock you in for years or impose a surrender penalty if you cash it in early. The surrender charge to get out of the annuity may be imposed for as long as 5 or 10 years. Variable annuities are great for the salesperson, but definitely not for the benefit of the owner. In Chapter 20, there is more discussion about annuities and the appropriate use of a fixed annuity in your retirement plan.

Mutual fund expenses will also reduce the return to investors.

Not all mutual funds are created equal. Some charge reasonable and modest fees to oversee your assets, while others may charge 8 or 10 times as much in expenses. Since most managed mutual funds do not attain the performance of their benchmark indices, it's important that you be aware of the expenses your fund is charging to "manage" your money. Don't overpay for "less than average" performance.

Rule 4 - You Gotta Get Serious

One thing Boomers have in common with Twenty-Somethings is that there is 24 hours in a day. Although time passes at the same pace for all of us, we become more aware of the passing of time as we age.

As we dream and plan for our future retirement, the time frame for accumulating retirement assets gets shorter. You have heard this before, but there is no better time to begin saving for retirement than right now. The sooner you get serious about setting retirement goals, developing an investment plan, and implementing that plan, the more flexibility you will have in choosing your retirement lifestyle.

Prior to entering the financial world, I worked in the Information Technology field. As a systems analyst, I learned to take many different elements (data, people, computers, information needs) and design a system to produce useful information (output). I set goals for the output and determined what information (data) would be useful in achieving those goals. I would then work backward and gather the data and resources necessary to achieve the goal. But the desired outcome had to be defined first.

If you have not already set goals for retirement, you have got to get serious about doing it now. The further you are from retirement, the more flexibility you have in setting those goals and greater is the probably of achieving your desired outcome. The closer you are to retirement, the more realistic the goal should be. That is, they should match the reality of your financial situation. If you are about to retire in a year or two, and your goal is to retire with five million dollars and live in a condo on the golf course, and you have only saved one hundred thousand dollars, you have a problem. Rereading Chapter 1 – Reality, might help give you some perspective on your situation.

Setting Goals for Retirement involves:

- Establishing goals for your retirement lifestyle.
- Preparing a budget to accommodate that lifestyle.
- Estimating retirement income from all sources.
- Determining how much savings and investments will be needed to generate that level of income. Set this amount as your retirement savings and investment goal.
- Setting periodic goals which will get you to that savings and investment goal by the time you retire.
- Making spending and savings adjustments as necessary to meet your periodic savings and investment goal.

The first step in creating and implementing a retirement plan is to take an assessment of your current financial situation. In Section 2, you will learn how to take a financial snapshot of what you are earning and spending, and the assets and debts which you currently have. You will also learn to establish a budget for pre-retirement asset accumulation or for spending and living in retirement.

For most of us, our retirement goals will emphasize the provision for life's basic needs, along with some of our wants. For example, housing, food, clothing, utilities, transportation, and medical needs are basic. Move past the basics into the area of wants, and we can add goals such as travel, recreation, entertainment, dining-out, and any number of other personal preferences. Our ability to meet these goals will vary depending upon the reality of our financial situation. The more time you have before retirement, the greater affect you can have on your financial situation in retirement. But you must get serious.

Chapter Questions

1. Why is it important to understand your emotions when making investment decisions?

2. What are the two emotions which all investors must recognize and deal with?

3. List 5 mistakes that investors should understand and avoid.

Chapter 3
Determine Your Cash Flow

Chapter Objectives

- Understand the purpose of a cash flow analysis.
- Itemize sources of income and expenses.
- Determine your cash flow.
- See your spending habits.
- Discover how much is available for saving/investing.

Why Prepare a Cash Flow Analysis?

Now that you have seen some of the issues you face as you plan and invest for retirement, it's time to get serious about developing your personal plan for *investing for retirement.*

If you are going to develop realistic investment goals and a plan for achieving those goals, you must know where your stand today… financially. You need to see how much you have available for saving and investing. It may be a worn out expression but it's important that you "don't get the cart before the horse." You can't plan a route to a desired destination if you don't know your starting point. Even with the best of intentions, you are not going to reach your savings goal if you don't have money left over each month after expenses are paid. You can't save and invest what you don't have.

Don't panic. You don't need a degree in accounting to see how much money you are taking in and where it is going. The information will come from sources you are already familiar with: your pay stub, check register, credit card statements, or checkbook software.

Preparing a financial snapshot is a crucial first step to developing a plan that will lead you to the retirement you desire. The first insight into your financial health comes from understanding your cash flow. That is, where your money comes from, where it goes, and how much is left over each month after the bills are paid. Essentially, this involves listing all of your sources of income (wages, interest, dividends, etc.) and expenses (mortgage, utilities, medical, credit cards, transportation, etc.). After paying your expenses, what you have left each month, if anything, is available for saving and investing.

I know you're thinking, "You really have a way of stating the obvious." But many people don't know where their money is going or if they are making any headway toward achieving their long-term wealth accumulation goals. Seeing the actual flow of our dollars and how we are spending them can be an eye-opening and traumatic experience for many.

Don't confuse a cash flow analysis with a budget. A cash flow analysis reveals the reality of your current earning and spending patterns—where your money is going. A budget is used to set goals or limits for your future spending. Once you see the reality of your current spending pattern, take it a step further and prepare a budget that will provide a surplus for savings and investing. You will never have a better opportunity to enhance your future retirement lifestyle than right now. The adjustments you make today to your spending habits, while you are still working, will have a significant impact on your lifestyle choices during retirement.

Prepare Your Cash Flow Analysis

The Cash Flow worksheet, in Appendix C, will help you categorize the items of income and expense. The key steps to preparing your Cash Flow Analysis:

- Review the worksheet in Appendix C to familiarize yourself with items of income and expense.

- Keep in mind, every financial transaction in your life can be categorized as income, expense, or savings/investment.

Before you begin the worksheet, gather your information sources such as your checkbook, bank statements, current payroll stub, and bills paid receipts. Last year's tax return may also be helpful.

If you find the detail of the worksheet to be too much, try using net or average numbers. For example, enter the net pay from your paycheck stub instead of the gross wages and all the payroll deductions.

However, try not to take shortcuts when entering the expenses. You need to include all the items which contribute to your cash outflow. If you find that you just can't deal with the detail of specific expense items, try totaling all the checks you have written for a three or six month period. Then enter the average monthly total as the Total Expense figure.

Some people find this task quite daunting while others revel in the detail of knowing how much is attributable to each item of income and expense. Don't let the detail hang you up. But keep in mind, the effort you put into determining the specifics of your current spending will help you later to develop more accurate spending, savings, and investment goals. This will become more important once you begin retirement when your options for adjusting your cash flow will be much more limited on the income side. It is the fortunate few who will have the same level of income in retirement that they had in their last few working years.

Income and expense categories:

Income: the all-inclusive list of your sources of income, earned or credited to your account—funds which are available for your immediate use. Do not include dividends, interest, or any amounts credited to accounts which are not available for immediate withdrawal, such as retirement accounts (if you are not yet taking distributions).

- Employment - wages and salary
- Savings and investments - interest and dividends; capital gains from sale of assets
- Social Security, retirement plan withdrawals, IRAs, 401(K)s, etc.
- Other sources of income - royalties or any other regular source of income.

Expenses: the all-inclusive list of your spending—where your money is going.

Fixed, non-discretionary expenses - little or no choice in spending

- Mortgage/rent payments
- Food
- Clothing
- Utilities
- Medical expenses
- Transportation
- Taxes
- Other expenses for needs.

Discretionary expenses - choices in spending

- Dining out
- Clothing accessories
- Entertainment/recreation
- Travel
- Subscriptions and memberships
- Miscellaneous spending.

Turn to Appendix C and prepare your Cash Flow Analysis. Remember, this is a list of your actual spending; it is not a budget for setting spending goals. If you are challenged or put off by numbers and worksheets, take a look at the *examples of completed worksheets* on the last few pages of Appendix C. The examples will give you an idea of what the completed worksheets should include.

Steps to preparing your Cash Flow Analysis:

1. Gather your information: check register, bank statements, bills paid, credit card statements, receipts, checkbook software income and expense printouts, etc.
2. Enter your income items: either in detail (gross with deductions) or net monthly amount. Be sure deductions such as medical insurance or taxes are not entered again in the expense section.
3. Enter your expense items: all expenses.
4. If you included any employer-withheld deductions for contributions to savings or retirement plans in step 2 above, enter those amounts also into the Additions to Savings & Investments section.
5. Enter any savings or investments you make directly into an account.
6. Total amounts for lines A, B, and C.
7. In the Net Discretionary Income Calculation table, fill in -

   Line 1: the amount from Line A (Total Monthly Disposable Income).

   Line 2: the amount from Line B (Total Expenses).

   Line 4: the amount from Line C (Total Addition to Savings & Investments).
8. In the Net Discretionary Income Calculation table, calculate -

   Line 3: subtract Line 2 from Line 1.

   Line 5: subtract Line 4 from Line 3.

The primary purpose for calculating your cash flow is to help you see your Net Discretionary Income and your spending. Your net discretionary income is what you have available to save and invest.

There is more discussion on the Cash Flow Analysis and it revelations, in Chapter 5.

Chapter Questions

1. Why was it important to prepare a Cash Flow Analysis? What did it reveal?

2. What are the two major categories for grouping financial transactions on a Cash Flow Analysis?

3. List examples of expenses by discretionary and non-discretionary categories.

4. Explain the different purposes of a Cash Flow Analysis and a Budget.

5. Did anything about your spending surprise you? Are these items for which you can adjust your spending?

Chapter 4
Determine Your Net Worth

Chapter Objectives

- Understand the purpose of a Balance Sheet.
- Know the role of financial assets in retirement.
- Prepare your personal Balance Sheet.
- See your debts in relation to your net worth.

Why Prepare a Balance Sheet?

Now that you have a clearer understanding of how much money is coming in and going out, you should see your financial habits more realistically. For some of you this may have been a cold shower; others may have gotten a warm fuzzy feeling. I suspect that for most, it is more the cold reality that "life is expensive."

To get a complete financial picture, one more snapshot will be helpful: your personal Balance Sheet and Net Worth statement. This will reveal your *current financial condition*. It will show you where you stand today with respect to achieving your financial goals for tomorrow.

The balance sheet will answer questions such as these: What financial assets do you have for generating retirement income? Do you have your debt under control? What types of assets have you accumulated? Are the majority of your assets appreciating or depreciating in value?

Preparing a balance sheet once a year will show you the reality of where you stand financially and provide perspective on your year-to-year financial condition. It will answer the question, "Are you meeting your financial goals as you prepare for retirement?"

That's the bottom line, the question you must answer, when *investing for retirement*. Will you have sufficient financial assets to spend during retirement or will you be dependent on Social Security for most of your income? The Social Security Administration says the average monthly Social Security benefit in 2010, was $1,164. If you were a high wage earner during all your working life, the maximum benefit for 2010 was $2,346 per month! You can do the math. Where will your retirement income come from? Will it provide the lifestyle you want?

Develop Your Personal Balance Sheet and Determine Your Net Worth

The Balance Sheet - Net Worth Worksheet, in Appendix C, will help you create a balance sheet and determine your net worth. Your personal balance sheet will list everything you own (your *assets*) and everything you owe (your debts or *liabilities*). Your assets minus your liabilities reveals your net worth—what you are worth financially.

Before you begin preparing the Balance Sheet - Net Worth Worksheet, a further explanation of the categories of assets and liabilities may be helpful.

Assets: the things you own or have a vested (ownership) interest in

- Cash, savings

- Investments
- Home
- Personal property
- Vehicles
- Retirement plans, etc.

Liabilities: what you owe—debts, financial obligations

- Home mortgage
- Vehicle and other loans
- Credit card debt, etc.

Net Worth: what remains of your assets, after all your liabilities are paid.

Do you begin to see the picture? What does your financial condition look like? I hope that your net worth is positive and you can see encouraging advances in your savings and investments from year to year.

However, some of you may find that your net worth is in negative territory—you are under water. It will take time and determination to right your financial ship and get back to a positive net worth. The determination to get your spending in line with your income and have money left over to pay off the debts can be a real struggle. If your income is ever reduced and your debts continue without any reduction, bankruptcy could become a reality. Most of us will experience a reduction of income during retirement, and retirement is no time for bankruptcy. If you have debt that is negatively impacting your ability to save and invest, I recommend that you check out Dave Ramsey's website (www.daveramsey.com) or tune in his daily radio or TV programs for help in developing a plan to achieve debt-free living. Mr. Ramsey's advice for budgeting and debt management are beyond the goals of this book.

Although it is not often put it in these words, let me say again: *It's your personal balance sheet that will determine your lifestyle in retirement.* If you are loaded with debt and have few assets to use to pay off the debt, you will be in for a lifestyle adjustment in retirement. This is another reason to take the time now to see where you stand, so that adjustments can be made while you are still in your wage-earning years.

A further word of caution is appropriate. Occasionally I find someone who wants to put unrealistic valuations on their assets, especially real estate. Another foundational truth that I was taught in 1983 during my rookie training was that **the value of an asset is exactly what someone else is willing to pay you for it... right now**. It is worth no more or no less—just what it will sell for now. In the years since that lesson, I have seen this truth play out many times in the financial and real estate markets. Our assets may have emotional value to us, but if we need to convert them into cash, they are worth only what we can sell them for today.

Keep that in mind as you place market values on your various assets. This net worth calculation is just for your eyes, and the more accurate and realistic it is, the better direction it will give you as you plan for the future. In valuing your assets, if you must err, err on the side of caution using conservative valuations.

Turn to Appendix C and prepare your personal Balance Sheet before continuing.

Chapter Questions

1. What information does a Balance Sheet present?

2. List examples of assets.

3. List examples of liabilities.

4. How is net worth calculated?

Chapter 5
Seeing Your Financial Reality

Chapter Objectives

- Understand your financial position today.
- Determine if you are a spender or saver.
- See your debts in relation to your disposable income.
- See the impact of debt on retirement savings.
- Draw conclusions from your personal situation.
- Estimate your retirement replacement income.

What Your Personal Statements Reveal

With your Cash Flow Worksheet and Balance Sheet in front of you, you now have an accurate picture of your *current* financial situation. The time you spent taking those financial snapshots will pay off when you begin to set your retirement goals and create a realistic investment plan.

The simple truth is, if you are spending more than you have coming in, you are either living off your assets, that is, consuming your savings, or you are piling up debt. There is no alternative. Mathematics works the same for all of us—Boomers, Twenty-Somethings, and retirees. If you find yourself spending more than you bring in, I urge you to get help with budgeting and controlling your spending. This book is not intended to be a guide to help you with budgeting, but a visit with a good financial counselor will help you see your current financial condition in realistic terms. As I previously mentioned, if debt is a problem for you, checkout Dave Ramsey's website (www.daveramsey.com) for advice and help with elimination of debt.

Let's take a look at the financial statements you have prepared.

Cash Flow Analysis

The Cash Flow Worksheet shows your income and how that income is being spent—where it is going. The Total Net Salary/Wages is your earned income from employment, after taxes are taken out. The Total Monthly Gross Income is what you have available to spend and save from all of your sources of income. This gross income figure has had the payroll deductions taken out and all other sources of income added in.

The expense categories reveal where you are spending your money. Did the actual dollar amounts for these items surprise you? When most people prepare this analysis for the first time, they are surprised to see where their money is going. One of the benefits of preparing a cash flow analysis is that it can identify hidden spending problems. Can you find items with amounts that are out of your comfort zone and make a determined effort to reduce your spending on those items?

Line C, Total Additions to Savings & Investments, is there to drive home a point. Relative to your spending, how much are you putting away in savings and investments each month? There needs to be something on line C, and the closer you get to retirement, the larger that number should be.

Line 3 of the Net Discretionary Income Calculation shows

what you have left after all spending is accounted for—your Net Discretionary Income after expenses.

Most financial worksheets will stop with this figure, the Net Discretionary Income. I want to emphasize the point about choosing to save and invest by including your current Total Additions to Savings & Investments. It's true that your Net Discretionary Income is what is available for saving and investing, but to get a picture of your real savings habit, look at the actual amount specifically *added* to savings and investments. The surplus or shortage on line 5 will get sucked into the spending side sooner or later. So make it a habit. If there is an amount on line 5, Net Monthly Surplus, deposit your surplus into a savings or investment account. Get it away from the accounts you use for spending—most likely your checking account.

Here is an additional thought for using the surplus: if you are comfortable with your addition to savings and investments and are on track to meet your financial goals, then use the surplus to occasionally treat yourself and family to something special. Life is uncertain. Enjoy the blessings of financial security that comes from the disciplined and prudent stewardship of your finances.

The Net Discretionary Income, line 3 on the Net Discretionary Income Calculation worksheet, will be used in the investment plan you are going to develop in Section 4 - Investing for Retirement. If there is no surplus, adjustments will be necessary to bring your spending in line with your income. You can't save and invest what you don't have.

Balance Sheet - Net Worth

The Balance Sheet - Net Worth worksheet paints a portrait of your financial health. It lists your assets (line TA), reveals what your spending and investing habits have accomplished, and shows where you are indebted (line TL). Line 3 of the Net Worth Calculation worksheet reveals your net worth—your accumulated financial wealth.

It's your net worth that you will draw on during retirement to meet the expenses which Social Security and employer sponsored retirement plans don't cover.

Using your personal balance sheet, you should be able to answer these questions:

1. Have you accumulated more assets than liabilities?
2. What type of assets have you acquired?
   Appreciating assets: home, savings, investments.
   Depreciating assets: vehicles, boats, personal property.
3. Do your assets have the potential to increase in value?
4. Is the level of your debt increasing or decreasing each year?

Draw Your Conclusions

Now let's bring this information together. With the Net Discretionary Income Calculation worksheet and your Balance Sheet in front of you, let's see what conclusions can be drawn from your current financial situation.

Use the following items of information:

1. Estimated *number of months* until you plan to retire.
2. The *Net Discretionary Income on line 3* from the Net Discretionary Income Calculation worksheet.
3. *Total Liabilities, line TL*, on your Balance Sheet.

Answer the following questions:

1. Do you have enough Net Discretionary Income (line 3) to pay off your liabilities (line TL) by the time you retire?
2. How long will it take to pay off all of your current liabilities? To calculate this, divide your Total Liabilities (TL) by the Net Discretionary Income (line 3). This gives you *an estimate of the minimum number of months it will take to pay off all your debts at your current income and spending level. Note: interest on the debt will also increase the number of months until pay off.*
3. Do you have enough Net Discretionary Income (line 3) to cover your current debt payments **and make additional contributions** to savings and investment accounts? What about additional payments to debt reduction?
4. What categories of spending can you realistically reduce in order to have, or increase, Net Discretionary Income as you move toward retirement?
5. If you begin retirement with debt, will you have enough retirement income to cover living expenses and make payments toward debt reduction? Use your estimated retirement income calculation, developed later in this chapter.
6. Are you in a job which will allow you to continue working

past your original estimated retirement date? How much longer could you work in your job if needed or desired?

7. Do you have 3 to 6 months of living expenses set aside in savings, such as CDs or money market accounts?
8. If you have Net Discretionary Income, are you maximizing the contributions to your IRA, 401(k) or other retirement plans?
9. Are there any anticipated future purchases that are not on the Balance Sheet as assets and debt liabilities and will impact the Balance Sheet? If so, do you have the future income to pay off this future debt before retirement? Have savings been set aside for this future asset purchase?

These are not easy questions for some people to answer. The reality of our past spending and saving habits is something we can't change. But we can make changes now which will affect our future spending and saving habits, and those changes will ultimately shape our retirement lifestyle.

If you have debt and available income for additions to savings and investments, I urge you to pay off as much of the debt as possible before you start retirement. One exception might be those who have a fixed mortgage on their home with ample income, now and in retirement, to cover the monthly payment. In that case, you would be paying off your mortgage with cheaper (future) dollars—dollars worth less in the future as inflation eats away at the purchasing power of those dollars.

Trust me on this, there will be no better feeling as you bungee jump into retirement than to know that you own your home free and clear.

Calculate Your Retirement Income

Another useful insight into your future retirement finances is seeing how much income you will need in retirement to replace your current take-home income.

To see this, take your current gross income and remove the various payroll deductions. This will show you the income needed in retirement to replace your current level of income. For example:

Gross Annual Income:	$90,000
Taxes on income (25%):	-22,500
Social Security:	-5,580
Medicare tax:	-1,305
Health insurance premium:	-3,600
Retirement plan contribution:	-4,500
Misc. other deductions:	-1,200
Current take-home income: (After taxes are paid)	$51,315

This example assumes a gross income of $90,000 and taxes (federal, state, local) at 25%. Taxes are taken out of this calculation because of the presumption that taxes in retirement will be different, possibly at a lower rate. Also, in retirement, you will not be paying Social Security, Medicare and medical insurance premiums at the same level, contributions to a retirement plan, and other deductions such as dues, life insurance, or disability insurance.

Now, let's calculate the approximate amount of income you will need in retirement to replace the take-home income you had during your working years. Using the table below calculate your information - **gross income needed in retirement**. You should adjust the tax rate on the income to reflect your specific state and local tax impact. Your replacement income needed should come from the cash flow analysis you previously made, or a retirement budget estimate you will make in Chapter 15.

	Example	Your information
Replacement income needed	$51,315(after taxes)	
Taxes on income	11,520 (18%)	
Medicare Part B	1,185 (rate for 2011)	
Gross income needed	$64,020	

The example revealed that you will need approximately 71% of your pre-retirement income during retirement in order to have the same level of spendable income. This is consistent with most replacement income calculations which range between 65 and 80 percent. I believe the lower end of the replacement range is realistic.

So where does your gross income come from? Fortunately there are several potential sources of income that you may draw on. The most notable of course is Social Security. During retirement you will also consume your savings and investments. That's what this book is all about—helping you save and invest for retirement income, so that you won't have to live at the subsistence level that Social Security provides.

To focus the picture on your specific circumstances, calculate your anticipated retirement income from information you currently have available. Use the statement you receive annually from Social Security and any bank, brokerage, or mutual fund statements, to fill in the information below. Compare this total anticipated income with your gross income needed calculation from above. This will show you the potential gap in your future retirement income.

Anticipated annual income from:

Social Security:	____________
Employer/union pension:	____________
Defined-contribution plan:	____________
IRAs:	____________
Interest from Savings, CDs:	____________
Dividends:	____________
Other:	____________
	____________
Total retirement income:	____________

You should now be able to see the connection between spending, saving, and investing, and the impact your spending habits will have on your future retirement income. If you have discovered spending habits which are keeping you from saving and investing at a level that will meet your goals, look for spending which can be reduced or eliminated.

Here are some suggestions which will help get you back on course to achieving your financial goals in light of your present financial reality:

1. Prepare a budget.
2. Set aside a specific amount each payday for savings or investment.
3. Look for expenses which can be eliminated altogether.
4. Eliminate credit card purchases which cannot be paid in full each month.
5. Pay off the highest interest debt first.

The balance of this book will lead you through the process of developing an *investing for retirement* plan that will fit your financial reality. As I have previously said, this will not be a one-size-fits-all saving and investment plan. Each of us approaches *investing for retirement* with different wants, needs, finances (income and debts), and temperaments. Your investment plan should be as unique and tailored to fit you as a custom-made suit. I'll lead you through the process of customizing your plan.

Chapter Questions

1. Did the cash flow analysis reveal any spending habits which surprised you?

2. Was there a consistent addition to savings & investments each month?

3. Define "Net Discretionary Income."

4. Did your Net Discretionary Income surprise you?

5. What insights did your Balance Sheet reveal to you?

6. What is the ratio of your appreciating assets to depreciating assets?

7. If you currently have debts, are they manageable and still allow for additions to savings and investments?

8. Will you have your debts paid off by the time you retire?

9. Calculate your retirement income. What did it reveal to you?

10. How much retirement income will you need to generate to replace your current level of income? Do you need to replace all of it? If there is a gap, what steps will you take to close it?

Chapter 6
Discover Your Risk Tolerance and Investing Temperament

Chapter Objectives

- Understand why investors buy stocks.
- Understand the connection between feelings and reactions.
- Determine your risk tolerance and investing temperament.
- Understand the three risk tolerance categories.
- Describe your risk tolerance category.
- Select an investment style to fit your comfort level.

Before jumping into the design phase of your investment planning, it is important to first discover your unique investing temperament. You need to understand how you react as an investor to events in the economic and financial world and how much risk you can tolerate.

The Tsunami of 2008/2009

When the Financial Tsunami struck in late 2008, everyone saw that financial markets can have periods of dramatic fluctuation! We witnessed the stock market take nail-biting plunges, then hopeful upward swings, followed by more heart-stopping plunges. It seemed that dismay and confusion were evident on the faces of everyone—politicians, economists, and stock market pundits alike. No one was able to offer a forecast that could survive the next plunge.

Some may question the behavior of the markets during those periods of extreme fluctuations, but the markets were behaving quite typically as they swung between basic investing motivations: fear and greed. Fear and greed can push our behavior to extremes. Because a market is a group of individuals coming together to buy and sell something, behavior of market participants can sometimes become volatile in the short-run.

As investors, we have a wide choice of investments for achieving long-term financial growth. The print and broadcast media are full of advertisements touting one great sure-fire investment after another—stocks, mutual funds, real estate, gold, annuities, you name it. "Look at the track record," they say; "it can't miss with a record like that." All these messages are designed to appeal to your emotions.

So how does an investor separate emotions from reasoned prudent decisions?

Your Emotions

Successful investors recognize that they have *investing emotions*—fear and greed. They understand that their emotions can interfere with their decisions.

Do you have your investing emotions under control? Are you aware of your emotions when they kick in? To help you understand this, let's review some recent events.

Leading up to the 2007 stock market peak, the real estate markets began to slow down and cracks appeared in the practice of house flipping. While house values were going through the roof, you could always find someone to unload the house on at a higher price than you had paid just a few months previously. But by early 2007, there were fewer buyers willing to take the house off your hands. Buyers who purchased houses with little down payment or cheap adjustable rate mortgages were desperate to sell and get out from under the mortgage. House prices buckled, then cracked, as real estate values fell in one area of the country after another. 2008 saw the collapse in house values spread across the nation, bringing values down as much as 40% or more in some areas. So much for the well promoted idea of easy wealth accumulation with real estate.

During that period, how were your investing emotions? Did you avoid the real estate bubble and take the much hyped gold route to "sound long-term financial survival?"

During the 2007-2008 stock market peak and crash, gold performed miserably. As the DJIA reached a new high, gold touched $1,000 an ounce. Then as the stock market turned down late in 2007, gold dropped to $900. By September 2009, after the markets began to recover and most indices were up 40 percent or more, Gold again crossed the $1,000 mark – providing not much more than a 10 percent advance.

Investors typically buy gold as an inflation hedge or as an alternative currency to the U.S. dollar for international commerce. Gold Bugs tout gold as a safe haven during political and economic uncertainty and stock market crashes. The reality is that gold trades more on emotion and speculation than on any underlying economic value. If you bought into the Gold Bug theory, you would have expected gold to increase in value as the markets were plunging and economic uncertainty was prevailing. In March 2008, gold traded for $1,004 an ounce. In the middle of the stock market crash of March, 2009, gold traded at $1,001, and by April 10, 2009, it was down to $882. During that 14-month period, gold had briefly dropped below $700. Money magazine reported in its May, 2009 issue that "gold has delivered lousy returns - on an inflation-adjusted basis, it's still trading far below its 1980 peak."[10] In 2010 gold had been as high as $1420, but after the North Korean attack on South Korea in November, gold was trading near $1,360. It was not trading as a hedge against political and economic uncertainty. It may be a commodity, but as an investment it is purely an emotional and speculative trade. Save your gold purchases for your jewelry.

During October and November of 2008, as the stock market gyrated 4 or 5% in a day, investors would be encouraged by news in the morning and an upturn in stock prices, only to be discouraged in the last 30 minutes of trading as stock prices headed south, dropping to new lows. The market did not play favorites, every sector and industry was impacted... negatively. Seasoned Blue Chips and newer growth stocks were both pummeled.

So let me ask, how were your emotions during that period of financial meltdown? Unless you were on mega-doses of medication, your emotions swung to the fear side. Mine did. I didn't like seeing my investment portfolio hammered and neither did you. Our normal human emotions reacted as they were designed to.

Let me be clear. You cannot be a successful investor by denying your emotions. In order to be successful, you must acknowledge and recognize those emotions and take determined action to prevent them from corrupting your investing decisions.

Markets fluctuate. They not only fluctuate daily, but financial markets, which are conducted through electronic media and disseminated worldwide instantaneously, fluctuate second by second. Don't let your emotions be manipulated by the moment-to-moment gyrations of the markets.

The only way I know to prevent this emotional manipulation is to take a long-term perspective for financial market participation. Remember, I said up front, this book is not for day traders—may they rest in peace. This book is for those of us who want long-term financial stability and growth in our assets as we invest for retirement.

Stock market investors, through the ownership of individual companies or equity mutual funds, must have a long-term perspective - at least a five-year commitment to the investment. The stock market is no place for short-term investing. It has provided an excellent and reliable return over time for patient investors, but as survivors of the Financial Tsunami can attest, it can be an emotional roller coaster in the short-term.

In spite of stock market cycles, stocks have outperformed bonds, gold, real estate, and other investment alternatives for periods of 20 years, 30 years or longer.

Investing Temperament

How will you feel when the inevitable market fluctuations occur? How will you react? The answers to those questions determine *your investing temperament.* Remember Rule 1- Know Yourself. Life is too short to set yourself up for anxiety or discouragement over your investments. You'll feel better and enjoy the benefits of a well thought out investment plan if you structure the plan to fit your temperament and emotional makeup. Designing a plan to fit your unique temperament will also increase the probably that you will stick with your plan—in both up and down markets.

Knowing your investment temperament and risk tolerance helps you structure a plan that will reduce your emotional reactions to stock market fluctuations. Remember, you can't make money in the market by bailing out and selling near a bottom when the outlook is darkest and your emotions are the gloomiest. Nor can you make money buying only when stocks are hitting new highs and everything looks fantastic for the future and you and everyone else are on an emotional high. Unbridled optimism and unchallenged confidence is a sure sign of a stock market top.

How Much Risk?

In addition to your risk tolerance, there are two other factors at work in determining how much risk you should take: the size of your investment portfolio and the number of years until you retire.

Obviously, an investor nearing retirement with a five million dollar portfolio, can afford more risk; i.e., potential for loss, than an investor with a two hundred thousand dollar portfolio. Multi-million dollar portfolios can afford to take greater risk with a portion of the assets, using investments such as the initial public offerings of young companies, leveraged investments, or hedge funds.

Hedge funds were riding high in 2007, only to be shot down in 2008. Recall the risk-reward concept—the higher the risk for loss, the greater the potential for reward. Using hindsight from the crash of 2008, let's rephrase the concept to this: the greater the potential for reward, the greater the risk of loss.

Since losses have a greater impact on smaller investment portfolios, less risk is advisable. However, all portfolios should incorporate some degree of stock market participation, and its inherent risk, in order to help minimize the impact of inflation.

The number of years you have before retirement also influences how much risk you should be taking. While younger investors have more time to make up for losses, 50-year-olds don't have that luxury. As our retirement date approaches, we need to shift into more *asset preservation* mode and less *growth* or *risk* mode.

Some people will fit into another group that I call non-investors. These people become too uncomfortable with market fluctuations to make any commitment to the stock or bond markets. They absolutely can't sleep knowing the value of their financial assets could decline tomorrow morning. These non-investors are making "no-risk" investments, primarily with CDs or short-term US Government bills that will generate no growth, and depending upon interest rate cycles, may also generate little income. They are taking a risk—the risk of inflation eating away at the purchasing power of their savings.

Is it hopeless for the non-investor? Of course not. If you find yourself in this group, you may be fortunate enough to have sufficient retirement income from an employer pension or Social Security. You might also have enough saved to continue your level of spending and not outlive your savings. Alternatively, you could choose to work longer or find a part-time job to supplement your savings. But keep in mind, the purchasing power of your savings will not keep up with inflation without some portion being invested in stocks, equity funds, or inflation-protected Treasuries. These investment choices are discussed in Chapter 9 - Selecting Investments. I have also included a model portfolio, the Insured Portfolio, in Chapter 10 - Model Portfolios, for those who are non-investors.

Risk Tolerance Evaluation

The purpose of determining your risk tolerance is to help you set an asset allocation (Chapter 7) which you can live with in both up and down markets. These personal characteristics determine the level of risk you and your investment portfolio can handle. They should be examined annually as you move closer to your retirement date to insure that you do not take a greater degree of risk than is appropriate or greater that you can comfortably live with.

It's important that you know your risk tolerance in order to develop an investment plan that you will stay committed to for the long-term.

To gain insight into your risk tolerance and investing temperament, take the evaluation using the Risk Tolerance Evaluation Worksheet in Appendix B. The worksheet is designed to help focus you on your emotional reactions regarding your savings and investments, and determine the risk level you should be taking with your investments.

Turn to Appendix B and complete the Risk Tolerance Evaluation Worksheet.

Let's examine what the evaluation revealed. The category you fit into measures your investing emotions and the level of risk you should be taking. One of these 3 categories should describe your risk tolerance:

Conservative - I am cautious about risking my investment portfolio and comfortable only with the degree of risk necessary to stay even with inflation.

Moderate - I am comfortable with some risk for the opportunity to grow my investments above the rate of inflation and can accept normal fluctuations in the overall value of my investment portfolio in order to achieve this growth.

Aggressive - I am a risk taker and not bothered by portfolio value fluctuations. I understand greater returns are possible only with greater risk—a higher potential for investment loss. I am comfortable with investing for maximum potential returns.

If you didn't fit comfortably into one of these three categories, you are not an investor. Your investing style and temperament is that of a saver. In the following chapters which describe asset allocation and selecting appropriate investments, you should choose CDs and federally insured investments. There is a fit for everyone.

Do you feel comfortable with the risk tolerance category the evaluation revealed? Does it surprise you? If it does, or you have doubts, maybe you answered more confidently than you really feel; you should pause here and review the evaluation.

Over the years most of my clients have been conservative or moderate risk-takers. It seems brokers and clients will gravitate to others with similar temperaments. During my active years as a broker and manager, I never developed a book of aggressive risk-taking clients. At the first office where I worked, the manager had a rule: never discuss commodities or other high-risk strategies with clients. He knew the typical broker is not trained or suited for high-risk customer care. If someone came in and wanted to trade commodities, they were to be immediately taken to the "animal farm," an area on the dark side where two brokers traded pork bellies and naked calls.

As we move closer to retirement we should move to a more conservative style of investing. Preservation of our financial assets becomes more important as retirement approaches. And once we retire, preservation of our assets is critical.

I prefer to present the risk tolerance and asset allocation concepts in terms that reference the *number of years until retirement*, instead of age. From an asset accumulation perspective, it does not matter how old you are when you retire. But once you retire, you no longer have the income from wages to add to savings and investments. Retirement abruptly changes the dynamics of earning, saving/investing, and spending.

However, our age is a factor when determining the amount of financial assets we will need for retirement. No one wants to outlive his/her savings. Will retirement last 15 years, 30 years or longer? We can't know this with any certainty. Fortunately, the date of our death is known only to God. But we can make a reasonable assumption for planning purposes based on our sex, health, family history, etc. Determining the number of years you will live in retirement is the most uniquely personal *estimate* you must make in this planning process. I counsel people to go for it—assume you will live well past what your family history might indicate. At a minimum, most 60- to 65-year-olds should plan on living in retirement for 30 years.

Chapter Questions

1. A predominance of equity (stock) investing is best suited for what period in our lives?

2. Why is understanding your risk tolerance and investment temperament important?

3. What two emotions can impact our success/failure as an investor?

4. Is it better to adjust your risk tolerance based on your age or your years until retirement? Why?

5. What are the three investor risk tolerance categories?

6. Into which risk tolerance category do you fit? Why?

7. Describe how you felt in 2008 and 2009 when the stock market was in decline, making lower lows, week after week. Did you react and make investment decisions? Did you stick with your investment plan?

8. With perspective on the Crash of 2008 and 2009, what lessons did you learn about the stock market? What lessons did you learn about your risk tolerance and investing temperament? What lessons did you learn about stock market recoveries?

Chapter 7
Establish Your Asset Allocation

Chapter Objectives

- Define asset allocation.
- Understand the role of asset allocation.
- Recognize factors affecting asset allocation.
- Learn the classes and sub-classes of assets.
- See the behaviors of each class of assets.
- Determine your asset allocation.

An important step in designing an investment plan is to determine how you will spread your financial assets among various asset classes. This is critical in both the accumulation and the retirement phases of investing. The proper allocation of assets is essential for the successful balancing of various dynamics such as your risk tolerance, the years until you will need to live off the investments, your need for income, and maintaining your future lifestyle from the purchasing power of your savings and investments.

You should now understand that in the world of investing…

- There are no free lunches.
- Your emotions can affect your investment results.
- Risk and reward are fundamentally connected.
- Your investments need to become more conservative as you move closer to retirement.
- In retirement, income and preservation of capital become primary objectives.

Asset Classes

How do you balance your need for income with growth of your investment assets so that your spending can keep up with inflation?

This is done with asset allocation—the spreading of your savings and investments across different classes of investments. Assets are divided into 3 classes:

- equities (stocks),
- fixed income (bonds), and
- cash equivalents (money market accounts, certificates of deposit, checking and savings accounts).

The purpose of asset allocation is to give your investment portfolio the balance between risk/growth and asset stability that is appropriate for your risk tolerance, years until retirement, and investing goals. Your asset allocation will fit your situation and will be different than your neighbors, co-workers, siblings, or children.

In this chapter you will determine your asset allocation based upon the following factors:

- **Years until retirement.** It is implied that retirement means the end of earned income. In retirement you are living off your investments, pensions, and Social Security, not wages. This key concept is presented as the years until your retirement, not your age. This provides a self-correcting factor since some people will choose to work longer, while others will retire earlier. The years available for accumulating financial assets is the key, not age.

- **Risk tolerance** - your style of investing. The three styles—conservative, moderate, and aggressive—are factors in determining the proportions of commitment to asset groups. Risk tolerance measures your comfort level with risk, a natural component of investing.
- **Investing temperament**. Your emotional response to financial market fluctuations will help fine tune your risk tolerance. Life is too short to be up at night worrying about your investments.

Let's look at the three broad groupings of asset classes: equities, fixed income, and cash equivalents. Each class has a place in a well designed investment plan. Each has a certain behavior, level of risk, and potential for return.

Equities are stocks, stock mutual funds, and stock ETFs. Equities represent participation in the capitalistic economic system through ownership of businesses as stockholders. They offer the greatest potential for appreciation of any asset class. Equities also expose our investments to a greater degree of risk than the fixed income asset class or money in the bank. It's a fundamental principal that over the long-term this greater risk offers the potential for greater return. But in the short-term (less than 5 years) the risk in equities increases and is greater than the other asset classes.

Fixed income is the class of assets which generates a stable flow of income to investors. This group is primarily bonds, bond funds, and other investments with a fixed rate of return. They offer predictable income, not growth of principal. Bonds are more stable in value than stocks because the rate of interest they pay does not fluctuate. The interest payment is set when the bonds are issued. Bonds can fluctuate in value as current interest rates move up and down, but the fluctuation is usually much less than stocks. Fixed income investments help provide stability to your investment portfolio.

There are factors other than the usual ebb and flow of interest rates, which may cause bonds to drop in value. For example, the issuer of a bond may get into financial trouble, which can create doubt that the bond principal will be paid back when the bond matures. For this reason, most investors should not try to pick individual bonds, but stick with bond funds or bond ETFs. With funds and ETFs, you have the safety of a diversified portfolio of bonds. Unless you are willing to spend the time to stay on top of your bond investments, leave the selection and oversight to the professional fund manager.

Cash, also called cash equivalents, is just that—cash in the bank. Cash equivalents are dollar denominated. Today this includes money in bank checking and savings accounts, money markets, certificates of deposit, and brokerage account money market funds. This is the portion of our financial assets which we can readily draw on for living expenses. The money is not at risk, and there is no principal fluctuation. A dollar deposited provides a dollar for withdrawal.

Each of these asset classes has an important place in our finances. Each class has certain characteristics that when taken together will help provide the growth, income, and stability we need in varying degrees in all the phases of our lives—working and retirement.

In summary, each asset class has its unique purposes and characteristics:

- Equities: provide growth, keep up with or ahead of inflation; principal will fluctuate.
- Fixed income: provide steady income; some stability of principal; can become less valuable due to inflation.
- Cash: provides liquidity; money for daily expenses; loses value to inflation.

The Financial Industry Regulatory Authority (FINRA) has developed an online Investor Knowledge Quiz[11] to test your understanding of the characteristics of the asset classes. It's designed to help investors understand the basics of investing and different behaviors of asset classes.

FINRA reports the following historical returns for equities and bonds over the last 80 years through 2007:

- Equities: 10.4% [12]
- Fixed income - Long-term Corporate Bonds: 5.9%[13]
- Fixed income - Long-term US Government Bonds: 5.5%

Remember, your particular asset allocation should change over time as you get closer to retirement. Growth of your investment principal is most important during your wage earning years while you are able to take more risk for a greater return. During your earning years, if an investment declines, you still have time to make up for the loss, something you are not able to do in retirement. A steady dependable stream of income from your financial assets is not as important during your working years as it will be in retirement. Therefore, as you move closer to retirement, your financial assets should shift toward a more conservative allocation with an increasing proportion of fixed income investments.

Over the years, one of the most common questions I am asked is, "Why should I invest in the stock market and risk losing my money, when cash in the bank, in long-term CDs, provides a guaranteed outcome." The answer is that the guaranteed outcome may not be sufficient to meet your income requirements. Consider a 4% CD, with inflation running at 3 percent and a modest tax rate of 15%. The interest you will earn is barely enough to cover inflation and taxes. This will leave you with inflation-adjusted, after-tax earnings of 40 cents on a $100 CD:

$100 CD @ 4%, interest earned =	$4.00
Inflation 3% of the $100 =	-3.00
Taxes 15% of the earnings ($4.00 x 15%) =	-.60
Inflation-adjusted, after-tax earnings =	.40

So how do investors position their financial assets for growth with appropriate levels of risk, income, and stability as they move toward retirement? These diverse and changing goals are achieved with **asset allocation**.

Determine Your Asset Allocation

The next step in designing your *Investing for Retirement* plan, is to determine your asset allocation. That is, determine the percentages of your total financial assets that you will allocate to each asset class: equities, fixed income, and cash equivalents.

To give you some perspective on where this discussion is headed, consider the following generic asset allocation for various age groups:

Age	Equities	Fixed Income	Cash
25	100%	0%	0%
40	85	10	5
50	60	35	5
60	45	50	5
65	35	55	10

This chart is intended only to give you a feel for how allocations need to adjust as you move closer to retirement. It does not factor in your individual risk tolerance, temperament, employment prospects, or years until retirement. It also makes an assumption that retirement is at age 65.

As the chart shows, Twenty-Somethings can and should be taking on greater risk in their asset mix. The 65-year-old retiree should have cash for living expenses readily available and investments oriented toward income and stability with a portion still invested in equities for growth. Please don't stop here. Your asset allocation may be quite different from this example.

Let's review. Fill in the following information which you previously developed:

- Years until retirement: ______________.
- Risk Tolerance (conservative, moderate, or aggressive): __________________________.

To determine *your unique asset allocation*, use the worksheets in Appendix D. The first worksheet, Table D-1, presents a general asset allocation mix. The second worksheet, Table D-2, will help you fine tune your specific asset allocation based on your risk tolerance.

Turn to Appendix D and complete worksheet D-1.

Understanding Your Asset Allocation

Using your personal parameters, risk tolerance, and years until retirement, you have determined your proper asset allocation using Appendix D.

As you move closer to your retirement date, you will need to periodically review your asset allocation. Your risk tolerance and investing temperament may not change, but the asset allocation should be adjusted by increasing the fixed income portion of your assets while reducing the amount in equities. I recommend that you set a specific date once a year for review of your asset allocation. Choose a date which is easy to remember such as your birthday. Once you have set a date for retirement, this annual review and adjustment becomes even more important.

Adjusting your allocation involves rebalancing the asset classes to match your allocation goal. For example, if the equity portion of your assets has risen to 55%, and your desired equity allocation is 45%, you must sell equities in an amount equal to 10% of your assets and invest that amount in fixed income and/or cash.

Notice that in Table D-2 the equity allocation is distributed by the size of the market capitalization of companies. Every company is placed in a market capitalization (cap) category (large cap, mid cap, or small cap). The market capitalization for a company is calculated by multiplying the number of shares the company has outstanding (held by investors) by the current market price of a share.

Market Capitalization = number of shares outstanding
x (times) current price of a share.

Large Capitalization (Large Cap): $10 Billion or more.
Mid Capitalization (Mid Cap): $3-10 Billion.
Small Capitalization (Small Cap): under $3 Billion.

Each of these three capitalization groups can have different behaviors within the general economic and stock market cycles.

> The Large Cap group is composed of more mature and stable companies. These companies offer greater price stability and potential for income distributions in the form of dividends. The price of their stock typically has less fluctuation.

> The Mid Cap group is composed of established companies, still growing but not as fast as in earlier periods. Mid Cap companies still need capital for growth so dividends, if paid at all, are not as generous as Large Caps.

> The Small Cap companies are growing and offer the best opportunity for stock appreciation, but also the greater risk. They are in need of capital for growth and may not pay a dividend, since all available capital is usually used for growth. The price of their stock will have greater fluctuations than the established Large Caps.

Equity investors seeking greater growth potential and little or no income invest in the Small Cap or Mid Cap equities. Investors seeking moderate growth and steady dividends choose the Large Caps.

The Fixed Income class of assets is composed of securities which offer a stream of regular income payments, such as bonds and preferred stocks. The interest paid on bonds does not change or fluctuate with the changes in interest rates. The interest rate on a bond is set at the time the bond is originally issued and is influenced by factors such as current interest rates in the market place and the credit quality of the issuing company or governmental entity.

Bonds and Notes issued by the United States Government are called Treasuries, They are backed by the full faith and credit of the United States Government. Treasuries are considered the highest quality of all securities. Because of their safety and assurance of being redeemed at maturity, they provide stability to the financial system and investors' portfolios.

Corporate bonds do not come with a government guarantee. A corporate bond is only as good as the issuing corporation's ability to redeem it at maturity. Corporate bonds come with a credit quality rating, ranging from investment grade (AAA) to junk bond (lowest grade). Unless you are willing to spend the time to research and evaluate bonds and the issuing organizations, you should not purchase individual bonds. Instead, investors should use mutual funds or ETFs for professionally chosen investment-grade bonds and for diversification of their fixed income investments in their portfolios.

Although fixed income investments offer more stability to a portfolio than equities, it's possible that there can be price fluctuations with bonds. This is called interest rate risk. When interest rates move up, the value of fixed income investments (bonds) moves down. The reverse can also happen. As interest rates go down, the value of bonds will move higher.

> *Why? Because the bond pays a fixed rate of interest regardless of the changes in interest rates. Therefore, your bond becomes more valuable when new bonds are issued with lower interest rates and less valuable when new bonds are issued with higher interest rates.*

There are exceptions to the rule that bonds are issued with fixed interest rates. Treasury Inflation Protected Securities (TIPS) (and a few corporate bonds) offer adjustable interest rates and principal, based on inflation indices. On adjustable rate bonds, as inflation increases, the interest rate will increase; when inflation subsides, the interest rate will decline.

In Appendix D, Tables D-3 and D-4, the fixed income asset class is divided into groups by duration, the time until maturity. The shorter the bond maturity, the less exposure to both interest rate and credit risk. Long-term bonds leave investors vulnerable to interest rate swings during the life of the bond.

Cash and cash equivalents are essentially money in the bank. *Cash equivalents* is a term that refers to money market accounts, savings accounts, and very short term CDs. These are accounts in which you deposit a dollar and get back a dollar plus any interest. The dollars in these accounts are vulnerable to a loss from inflation—a reduction in the purchasing power of those dollars. However, these accounts do provide safety and a convenient method for paying bills. For retirees, these accounts provide a level of comfort knowing there is money in the bank. However, for younger investors who face years of inflation and must keep their financial assets growing, keeping excessive cash reserves can be a mistake. Only during a period of deflation will cash become more valuable. Historically, periods of deflation have been short-lived.

You should now understand that…

- Asset classes are used to achieve investing goals.
- Asset classes have different behaviors and purposes.
- Your risk tolerance is important in determining your Asset Allocation.
- Your asset allocations will shift over time.
- As you move closer to retirement, your Asset Allocation should become more conservative with increased emphasis on fixed income investments.

Occasionally, someone will tell me he is uncomfortable with the allocation mix that I recommend. If you are uneasy about the allocations determined in Appendix D, you should refine the mix to a more conservative posture to accommodate your investing temperament. Maybe you're more risk averse than you think. As I have said, life is too short to worry about your investments. Don't set yourself up for failure before you get started, using an investment structure that you can't live with. Don't choose an allocation that will send you to the exit to cash out at the first sign of market fluctuation.

If your investing temperament does not handle risk well, use a more conservative mix by reducing or eliminating the equity portion of your allocation. Keep in mind, that as you become more conservative (or risk averse), you will be reducing the growth of your financial assets and, therefore, the amount of financial resources to draw on in retirement.

If you are unsure about determining an asset allocation and selecting mutual funds or ETFs for your retirement plan, or find the process somewhat intimidating, hang in here. In Chapter 10 - Model Portfolios, I offer three portfolios with recommended funds for your investing plan.

Chapter Questions

1. How many asset classes are there? Name the different asset classes.

2. What is Asset Allocation?

3. Do all classes of assets provide the same level of risk and return? What are the historical returns on equities and fixed income?

4. What does asset allocation do for the investor?

5. What are the three factors in determining your asset allocation?

6. What are the three categories of assets within the equities class?

7. How do the three equity categories differ?

8. What are the fixed income categories? How do they differ?

9. How is the asset class *cash equivalents* best utilized?

Chapter 8
Tapping Investment Expertise

Chapter Objectives

- See the advantage of using professional expertise.
- Know how our emotions may affect our investing judgment.
- Understand the advantages of using mutual funds and ETFs.
- Learn the role of diversification.
- Understand the impact of fund expenses.
- Evaluate the performance of an investment against a standard.

The Case for Professional Management

In the previous chapter, you were guided to an investment asset allocation which fit your unique temperament, situation, and goals. Using those asset allocation percentages, you will select mutual funds and ETFs that match your asset allocation classes and leave the specific investment choices to the professional fund managers.

Think about it. Do you have the level of interest to devote to investment research and selection? Do you want to spend the time to research and stay on top of your stock selections? Can you devote the time to research, reading, and communication with company management? Do you have the investment knowledge to spot gems or turkeys among the tens of thousands of investment opportunities?

If you are like most people, you do not. Why should you spend the time and take the financial risk? Do you go to a doctor for medical treatment? A mechanic for automotive repairs? A computer geek for computer advice? Of course you do.

Then why not also turn to professionals for investment selections? It may not be as much fun as picking a stock and watching it double in a short time, confirming your investment genius, but it is certainly more fun than picking a stock and watching it drop like a rock, also confirming your investment genius. For most people, leaving the oversight to professionals makes it easier to sleep at night. It certainly will improve your potential for achieving your investment goals.

Do you recall the financial headlines and stories in 2008 when the stock market was entering a Bear Market? A Bear Market occurs when the market indices fall 20% or more from the previous high. In July 2008 both the DJIA and the Standard & Poor (S&P) 500 Index had fallen by more than 20% from their October, 2007 highs. The *experts* were all over the map predicting the bottom of the market downturn or maybe a bounce before a further fall, known as a Bear Market rally. Which view did you believe? They both sounded logical. Should you jump back into the market or stay out and not suffer further losses if the market continued to head down? One course of action was motivated by greed, not missing a buying opportunity; the other course was motivated by fear, the worst is yet to come!

July 2008, was a time when investors needed to understand Rule 1 - Know Yourself. What will you do in a Bear Market? Will you panic along with the investors shown on the evening news, or stay the course, commit to your long-term investing plan, check your asset allocation, and ride out the inevitable market cycles?

A fundamental market principle that investors must recognize is that a Bear Market will not end until there is "Capitulation." This occurs when there is nothing but bad news on the investing front, and investors give up on stocks and mutual funds, throw in the towel, and sell their shares. This creates extremely high volume of sales as stock prices go into a free fall. Many investors become completely discouraged and end up selling as stocks near a Bear Market low. This is the worst possible reaction—selling at the low.

You can't make money investing by selling low and buying high. As obvious as that statement may seem, it is easy to forget this truth when our emotions kick in during times of either market euphoria or despair.

So again, I ask, "How will you react to a Bear Market and emotional turbulence?" With a well thought out investment plan and understanding your investing temperament (emotions), you can stay on track and minimize the potential for serious investing mistakes in the heat of the moment.

Using Mutual Funds and ETFs

Of all the investment choices available to investors, the mutual fund and exchange-traded fund (ETF), when purchased at periodic intervals, offer the best mechanism for attaining financial goals. In one investment package you get all the advantages that have proven essential for wealth creation: diversification, professional investment oversight, and the opportunity for wealth accumulation, previously available only to wealthy individuals.

By ourselves, we do not have the resources to analyze companies, industries, and markets for a sufficient number of companies to achieve proper diversification. The cost advantage of using mutual funds and ETFs is also very compelling. Funds are able to buy and sell the securities in their portfolio more cheaply than individual investors. Competition among investment firms for investors' assets has helped keep many funds management fees very low.

However, let the investor beware, not all funds are inexpensive or successful. Some funds can be off the chart with excessive expenses, while producing only mediocre results.

In the last few decades, mutual funds and exchange-traded funds have become the primary investment choice for most investors. Let's examine them more closely.

Definition of a mutual fund: an investment fund which buys and holds securities, such as stocks or bonds, and sells units or shares of the fund to the investing public. The fund is managed by an investment firm such as Fidelity Investments, Vanguard, Merrill Lynch, USAA, or Charles Schwab among many others. The mutual fund manager is responsible for selecting all the individual stocks or bonds in the mutual fund's portfolio. The manager of a *managed mutual fund* makes decisions such as how long to hold an investment, when to sell the investment, and how much cash to keep on hand. *Indexed mutual funds and ETFs* are composed of investments that reflect an established index of stocks or bonds. In an indexed fund, the manager does not decide which investments to buy; the fund will own only the securities that are in the index.

Typically, a mutual fund has a specific investment style and fits in an asset class category such as large cap fund or intermediate-term investment grade bond fund. The classifications of mutual funds are as diverse as there are types of investments. Investors own shares of the fund which are valued at the same price per share regardless of the number of shares the investor owns—equal treatment for all investors. The mutual fund manager reports the total value of the fund, number of shares outstanding (owned by investors), and the value of each share, every afternoon after the close of the New York Stock Exchange. Mutual funds will sell shares to investors every day at the daily determined price. The fund will also redeem (cash out) shares daily at the afternoon price. This provides a public and liquid market for the shares of the mutual fund. These types of mutual funds are also known as open-ended funds, because they are constantly selling and redeeming shares.

The primary advantages of mutual funds are…

- Diversification.
- Professional selection of the investments, such as stocks, bonds, and cash.
- Pooling of many investors' money to achieve low expenses.
- Liquidity - they are easily bought or sold by large and small investors alike.

Definition of an exchange-traded fund (ETF): similar to a mutual fund, but it is bought and sold by investors like a share of stock on a stock exchange; it is not sold or redeemed by the managing investment firm. The ETF holds a portfolio of investments, stocks, bonds or commodities, which represent an index, such as the S&P 500 Index®. An ETF could also represent a style of investment, such as Small Cap Growth or Total Bond Market. Usually the portfolio is composed of a strict set of investments which match an index or other fixed, non-managed, pool of securities. This non-managed portfolio gives the ETF a major expense advantage over managed mutual funds. Some ETFs have expense ratios as low as .07%, with many in the .15% - .25% range.

An ETF's shares are traded on a stock exchange; the price is determined by the market (buyers and sellers), not the underlying value of the investments in its portfolio. The ETF may trade above or below its true investment portfolio value. This isn't a problem since large investors and investment companies are able to immediately buy and sell large blocks of shares, known as creation units, whenever the ETF strays from its true underlying portfolio value. This ability to immediately buy and sell helps keep the ETF close to its true asset value.

Recently new ETFs have been introduced that are designed to contain *managed portfolios*. That is, the ETF manager makes decisions regarding which investments the ETF should hold. These ETFs do not match a pre-selected pool of investments such as an index. It's not yet clear how these managed ETFs will perform or if they will be able to match a key advantage of traditional ETFs: low expenses.

Beware that as ETFs become more popular, new ones are coming out with more exotic investment themes. Some are industry specific, highly leveraged (borrow money to buy the investments), or may be a contrary play on the direction of an industry. That is, the ETF will move up in price as the pool of securities it follows declines in price. This is a high-risk strategy and one I do not recommend for anyone who is *investing for retirement*.

Also note that recently some bond ETFs have had trouble delivering the returns investors expect from an ETF which tracks a particular bond index. This can occur when the ETF is unable to purchase bonds to match the index. That is, the underlying bonds are not available during volatile markets or the bonds themselves are lightly (infrequently) traded. Usually this is not a problem, but if you are concerned about the possibility, consider a comparable mutual fund as an alternative investment.

When selecting an ETF, be sure it has average to high daily trading volume and at least fifty millions dollars in assets. Some of the newer, narrowly focused ETFs have recently closed due to low investor interest. All of the ETFs listed in Appendix E have a traditional investment style with sustainable trading volumes.

The primary advantages of exchange-traded funds are…

- Diversification.
- Very low expense costs.
- Liquidity—trade on an exchange like stock so they can be bought or sold quickly.
- Easy to select one which matches a specific investment style or index.

There are other types of investment companies from which investors may select. These have been around for decades, although they are not as popular today as mutual funds and ETFs.

- Closed-end fund: an investment company which has sold a fixed number of shares in an initial public offering. The shares trade on an exchange or market as one owner sells to another. The investment company does not redeem or issue shares. These funds may be actively or passively managed and can pay dividends to owners periodically. These older funds are similar to today's ETFs.

- Unit investment trust: an investment company which has sold a one-time offering of shares, called units, to the public. The units may trade on a market but will have a fixed life or date for redemption by the investment company.

Diversification

The dictionary defines diversification: "to make diverse, to distribute among different kinds of securities." From an investing perspective, it also means to spread the risk among many investments.

Diversification is a foundational principle of good financial stewardship. Diversification not only requires owning many companies, but owning companies spread across different industries. In today's financial environment, diversification also calls for the ownership of foreign companies. It's the essence of not having all of your eggs in one basket, industry, or country. Diversification provides stability to your portfolio; when one investment or group declines, the other companies or groups can help to offset the decline.

In its broadest sense, diversification means diversification by…

- Asset class: equities, fixed-income, cash equivalents.
- Industry sector.
- Market capitalization.
- Domestic and foreign.
- Credit quality.
- Fixed-income maturities.

A well-diversified equity mutual fund or ETF may have several hundred or more companies in its portfolio. However, there are some excellent funds which own as few as fifty companies and some with 500 or more. The prospectus for the Vanguard Total Stock Market Index Fund (VTSMX) states, "The Fund typically holds 1,200–1,300 stocks in its target index (covering nearly 95% of the Index's total market capitalization) and a representative sample of the remaining stocks." That means as the stock market goes, so goes this fund—it has covered all the domestic capitalization categories, large to small.

As a fund increases the number of companies it owns and begins to approach the total stock market in ownership diversification, the performance will begin to move toward the historic average annualized return for equities of approximately 10.5%. Funds owning a fewer number of companies are more likely to experience greater average annualized returns, either positive or negative.

A significant advantage of the mutual fund and ETF is that they offer *safety through diversification*. Diversification is critical to sustained long-term growth for all investors, large or small, conservative or aggressive. It helps to moderate the swings in the economic cycles while providing the investor with the needed balance between risk and reward.

There is no better means for the small investor to maintain an equal footing with wealthy investors and pension funds, and to achieve diversification, than owning a mutual fund or ETF.

Watch Expense Ratios

A fund's expense ratio indicates what you are paying annually for the management of the fund. It's calculated as the ratio of the fund's total expenses to the fund's total assets, expressed as a percentage.

Many index oriented mutual funds and ETFs have rock bottom expense ratios, usually less than .25%. A few ETFs have expenses as low as .07%. When mutual funds and ETFs with similar investments and styles are compared, those with the lower expenses almost always have better long-term total returns. Expenses do matter when it comes to the return to the investor.

Understandably, the management expenses of managed mutual funds are greater than those of index funds. An index fund only needs to invest in a portfolio of securities that will match a predetermined index. Index fund managers can automate much of the investment process.

The manager of a managed fund must make decisions concerning which stocks or bonds to purchase. This requires a staff of analysts who evaluate investments and make recommendations to the manager. The additional expense burden for managed fund managers can be quite substantial.

I think it is quite reasonable to expect professionals to be compensated for their efforts, especially when their investment selections produce better than average returns for the investor. But investor beware! Some of the highest expense funds have the worst annualized returns. Many of the managed funds have expense ratios between 1 and 2 percent. There are some funds which unashamedly charge more than 2 percent. The impact of expenses on your investments can be significant, especially for long-term investors.

Scott Burns, the Dallas Morning News personal finance columnist, offers this advice regarding high expenses for long-term investors: "The best long-term strategy is cost reduction."[14]

For example, look at the impact of fees on two managed mutual funds over a 20-year period. The initial investment in each fund was $50,000. The assumed annualized rate of return is 10.5%, which is close to the S&P 500 Index® annualized return over the last 20 years. Observe the difference in the value of the two investments after 20 years:

Initial investment value	$50,000

After 20 years, the investment value with a 10.5% annual return:

Fund A with a .58% expense ratio	$327,800
Fund B with a 1.58% expense ratio	$276,840

The difference between these two funds is $50,960. That's your money. Your savings can be even greater when you use low expense index mutual funds or ETFs.

To observe the impact expenses can have on your funds, go to the Securities and Exchange Commission web site, www.sec.gov/investor/tools/mfcc/get-started.htm, and use their Cost Calculator. You can enter parameters such as the number of years for holding a fund, expense ratio, and the anticipated rate of return into the calculator.

The mutual funds and ETFs mentioned in this book have expense ratios of less than 1%.

Measurement of Performance

How do you know if your fund is producing an above average return? Compare it against a benchmark. A generally accepted measurement in the financial community is to compare the fund's return against an index in its investment category, such as large cap or small cap indices.

A financial index is a statistical *measurement* of a group, or universe, of financial instruments (stocks or bonds), which can be easily determined daily; i.e., an index of large capitalization stocks, small capitalization stocks, investment-grade bonds, or of whatever grouping you want to take a reading. These readings, called the index, are usually calculated on a daily basis. However, with today's computer technology, most indices are calculated in real-time and reported every few seconds.

A large capitalization mutual fund's performance is measured against the Standard & Poor 500 Index®. Did the fund beat or trail the index after expenses are taken out? The comparisons should be viewed from the perspective of the last 12 months, 3, 5 or 10 years. Don't get sidetracked with 3-month or short year-to-date comparisons. Even top performing funds do not hit home runs every day.

A sad reality is that on average, most managed mutual funds have underperformed their benchmark indices! As The Wall Street Journal pointed out, there is "clear evidence from studies that index funds tend to outperform their actively managed rivals."[15]

S&P, the keeper of numerous stock market indices, reported[16] on the dismal state of performance by active investment fund managers for the 5-year period ended December 31, 2008. The S&P indices outperformed the managed funds by wide margins: 71.9% of the large-cap funds, 79.1% of the mid-cap funds, and 85.5% of the small-cap funds.

Don't pay for less than average performance. There are a number of good performing, managed funds, with expense ratios under 1 percent. I believe most investors would be best served sticking with low expense index funds and ETFs.

Remember, trying to pick a top performing fund based upon current or past performance is a fool's game. Instead, look at the fund's sustained performance over the past 5 or 10 years. Also check to see if the manager who generated that past performance is still there.

Here are some useful benchmarks you should use when comparing your fund's performance:

- Large Cap Index: S&P 500 (Standard & Poor 500®); 500 largest US companies.
- Mid Cap Index: Russell Midcap Index®; 800 companies with $8-10 billion

capitalization.

- Small Cap Index: Russell 2000 Index®; 2000 companies with under $3 billion in capitalization.
- Mid-Small Cap Index: Russell 2500 Index®; 2500 small and mid cap companies with up to $10 billion of market capitalization.
- Foreign Index: MSCI EAFE® - Morgan Stanley Capital International Europe Australasia & Far East; composed of 21 global indices; global stock measurement.
- Total US Stocks Index: Dow Jones Wilshire 5000 Index®; measures total US stock market with over 6500 stocks in the index.
- US Bond Market Index: Barclays Capital US Aggregate Index®; formerly Lehman Aggregate Bond Index; measures total US bond market.

This is not an exhaustive list of indices. The financial community has invented numerous others and offshoots of these to measure stock and bond performance. These are the most widely followed and reported measurements.

In 2009, Dow Jones & Company introduced the Dow Jones

Real Return Target Date indices. Dow Jones described them as "a family of rules-based indices designed to measure the performance of lifecycle portfolios that seek to grow and preserve real value over time." In other words, these indices will adjust over time to match the needs of individuals for capital preservation and growth of their retirement assets. These indices will also measure the performance of inflation-protected securities, real estate, and commodities, in addition to the traditional measure of equities and fixed-income investments. For target date and lifecycle investors, these indices should provide a better measure to judge their funds against.

Other useful tools you can use for fund performance measurements are the fund rating services Morningstar and Lipper. These independent rating services each perform measurements and analysis of mutual funds based upon their own criteria such as total return performance, tax efficiency, or preservation of capital. They rate a fund on a comparison scale to other funds in the same category.

Morningstar provides a star rating for a fund, comparing it to peer funds in the same category that the fund is assigned. *Five star* is the highest, *one star* is the lowest rating Morningstar assigns. Morningstar categories include large value, small growth, or moderate allocation among numerous others. Morningstar also assigns each fund to a style profile which it describes as a summary of the fund's risk factor exposure, such as capitalization size, value or growth orientation, and historical return volatility among many other style factors. The star rating is of interest when evaluating a fund against its peers in the same category. It is not a rating for comparison to all funds regardless of asset class or category. Morningstar has also recently introduced a target date fund index measurement. For more information on Morningstar's ratings, go to their web site, www.morningstar.com.

Lipper uses a numeric scale of 5 (highest) to 1 (lowest) in each of 5 measurement categories: total return, consistent return, preservation, tax efficiency, and expenses. For additional details, go to their web site, www.lipperweb.com, then choose their Fund Screener. Using the screener you can enter criteria such as asset type (equity, bond, etc.) or classification of assets which the fund owns (United States, global, sector, value, core, or growth orientation, among many other selectable criteria). These ratings help you see your fund from several perspectives.

Should You Use an Advisor?

Sometimes people just don't have the interest or personal commitment to handle their own investments. They may have given it a try and experienced financial losses and trauma which they swore they would never again inflict on themselves. Or occasionally the investment choices may seem so overwhelming, people freeze and are unable to make a decision. If you feel you may fall into this group, I encourage you to hang in here and read the rest of this book – it will provide you the foundation for creating your plan. You can do this. You can do this well, and with guidance and information you can achieve your financial goals.

However, if you feel that you just can't manage your investments or plan, consider using an advisor. There are several names for people who help others with their investments and financial goals and plans. They are called advisors, planners, consultants, or counselors. Sometimes brokers, agents, or investment representatives are also acting as advisors. Don't get hung up on the title.

If you decide to use someone for advice/counsel/planning, keep in mind the following guidelines:

1. The advisor should listen to you. If you feel he/she is not listening or asking your opinion, get out. This is not the advisor/planner for you.
2. You need to be open and honest with the counselor. Express you desires, goals, time frame, and accurate financial situation. Discuss your investing emotions, temperament, and tolerance for risk, or lack thereof.
3. You must feel comfortable with the planner. If he is not a match for your personal tastes, don't try to force a change on either of you. If he has a system for stock picking and you are more conservative or a fund investor, this will not be a good fit.
4. Know what you want from the advisor before you initiate a first visit.
5. Be sure the counselor is accessible. Does she return phone calls? How timely?
6. Ask about compensation. How is she paid? A counselor/advisor/planner/broker will be focused on the person/firm/investment who is compensating him/her.

7. Understand that advisors/planners/counselors/brokers are compensated several different ways:

    Fee only - you pay for advice; hourly or per investment plan; does not sell the investments recommended.

    Manage portfolio - charge percentage of portfolio assets; ranges from .6 - 1.25%.

    Broker or agent - per transaction to buy/sell securities or percentage of portfolio.

    Combination - fee plus commission.

    Performance based - percentage of return on the portfolio.

8. Ask them how they became an advisor. What qualifies them to advise you?

Chapter Questions

1. How do many investors react when bad news hits the stock market?

2. What is the best investment for small investors that will offer equal footing with large investors?

3. List four advantages of mutual fund or ETF investing.

4. How is a mutual fund share price calculated? How frequently?

5. What determines an ETF's share price? How frequently?

6. What is the primary difference between a managed fund and an index fund?

7. What is the correlation between a fund's expense ratio and its performance?

8. List several firms which provide mutual fund rating services.

9. List several ways that brokers, counselors, planners or advisors are compensated.

Chapter 9
Selecting Investments

Chapter Objectives

- Understand the role of your personal investing profile.
- Understand the meaning of your Total Portfolio.
- Practice making investment selections for different case studies.
- Make your personal investment selections.

Before focusing on the selection of the investments which fit your investing goals, let's review the information you have developed so far concerning your unique risk tolerance, temperament, and asset allocation.

These personal factors should fit you like a glove. If you are uncomfortable with any of them, revisit the previous chapters and refine your profile to fit your comfort level. Don't try to force yourself into an investing style which you find uncomfortable and will be unable to stick with.

So far, you have developed your personal information profile to reveal…

- Personal Cash Flow Analysis (Chapter 3).
- Cash available monthly for savings and investing (Chapter 3).
- Personal Balance Sheet (Chapter 4).
- The number of years/months until you retire.
- Your risk tolerance and investing temperament (Chapter 6).
- The best asset allocation to match your profile (Chapter 7).

While I encourage all investors to inform themselves about their finances and investments, I do recognize that not everyone is comfortable making financial and investment decisions. If you are challenged and outside your comfort zone as you try to understand your investment profile, asset allocation, and investment choices, don't panic. In the next chapter, I have included several model portfolios for you to use to help eliminate your anxiety about making investment selections. Chapter 10 - Model Portfolios, offers three investment portfolio allocations, each with pre-selected investments. One portfolio is for everyone who is still working and *investing for retirement*, another is for retirees, and a third is for people who are savers, not investors.

However, I strongly encourage you to read through this chapter for a better understanding of the portfolio selection process. It's not rocket science. It's the application of investment principles guided by your risk tolerance, temperament, time until retirement, and goals.

Calculating Your Total Portfolio

The process of selecting your investments is driven by your asset allocation, not the size of your investment portfolio. This process will allocate the investment amounts among mutual funds and ETFs, as *percentages of your total portfolio*.

Your *total portfolio* is the total of your financial assets, all accounts over which you have control. These accounts include…

- Cash and savings in the bank
- Certificates of Deposit

- IRAs - traditional and Roth
- Retirement accounts - 401(k), 403(b), etc.
- Brokerage accounts
- Stocks, bonds, mutual funds, ETFs, etc.

Your total portfolio does not include accounts for which you do not make the investment decisions, such as employer paid pensions, Social Security, and trust funds. Even though you may have vested ownership in these accounts, you have no control over how they are invested.

To see the full picture of your current *Total Portfolio*, that is, the total financial assets which you control, complete the table on the following pages.

Financial Asset	**Current Value**	**Asset Class**
Checking Accounts		Cash
Savings Accounts		Cash
Money Market Accounts		Cash
Certificates of Deposit		Cash
Taxable Brokerage Accounts:		
Stocks, equity mutual funds, ETFs		Equity
Bonds, bond mutual funds, ETFs		Fixed Income
Cash, money market funds		Cash
Other:		

IRAs:		
Stocks, equity mutual funds, ETFs		Equity
Bonds, bond mutual funds, ETFs		Fixed Income
Cash, money market funds		Cash
Retirement Accounts 401(k), 403(b)...		
Stocks, equity mutual funds, ETFs		Equity
Bonds, bond mutual funds, ETFs		Fixed Income
Cash, money market funds		Cash
Mutual Funds (not held in brokerage accounts):		
Equity funds and ETFs		Equity

Bond funds and ETFs		Fixed Income
Money market funds		Cash
Other financial assets:		
Total Portfolio		

Be sure each financial asset is assigned to its asset class (Equity, Fixed Income, or Cash).

The following example is a snapshot of a portfolio's asset allocation:

Example Asset Allocation

Asset Class	**Current Value**	**Percentage of Total Portfolio**
Equities	$52,100	52%
Fixed Income	43,000	43%
Cash Equivalents	4,900	5%
Total Portfolio	$100,000	100%

Take a quick snapshot of your current portfolio's asset allocation. Use the table on the next page to calculate the total of your financial assets - for each of the three asset classes using the information from the previous table. Then calculate the percentage of each class relative to your Total Portfolio:

Current Asset Allocation

Asset Class	**Current Value**	**Percentage of Total Portfolio**
Equities		
Fixed Income		
Cash Equivalents		
Total Portfolio		100%

This table reveals your current portfolio asset allocation. How does it compare to the asset allocation you selected in Chapter 7? Were you surprised by your actual allocation? The annual calculation of your asset allocation is an important step to help you stay on course and achieve your financial goals for retirement. There is more discussion in Chapter 12 about rebalancing your assets to match your desired asset allocation.

Case Examples for Selecting Investments

Now, let's look at the process of selecting the investments for your portfolio. This is a **four-step** procedure which ties together your profile, the Asset Allocation Tables in Appendix D, and the investments in Appendix E.

For illustration purposes, I have developed four case examples. To help you understand the individualized process of selecting appropriate investments, each case uses three variables: total portfolio amount, risk tolerance, and number of years until retirement. Work through each of the four cases which follow, using Appendix D and E for investment selections.

Remember, the purpose of this exercise is to help you see the *process* for developing a retirement plan and selecting investments that match different tolerances and goals. After understanding how this process works, you should be ready to develop a plan for yourself. Following Case 4, the steps are listed that will assist you in developing your plan.

> Note: I have included in these portfolio examples an inflation-protected U.S. Government Bond mutual fund. My reasoning for including this type of investment is: in the post-2008/2009 Crash environment, the U.S. Government has flooded the economy with money. Although politicians seem unable to agree on what to call it, they have agreed to spend taxpayer money to fund it. But regardless of what it is called—bailout, tax-cut, stimulus, TARP, quantitative easing, or rescue—the result is the same: the country is awash in cash, credit stimulus, and

government guarantees. And unless the Federal Reserve and the Obama Administration are very skilled and fortunate, this cash infusion will lead to increased inflation in the next few years.

Case #1

Years until retirement: **10**

Risk tolerance: **Moderate**

Portfolio size: **$100,000**

Step 1 - Select the years until retirement and risk tolerance.

Return to the Asset Allocation Tables in Appendix D, where you determined your asset mix based on your investor profile: risk tolerance, temperament, and years until retirement. On Table D-1, find the columns which match the years until retirement and risk tolerance. The column reveals the percentage allocation for each asset class: equities, fixed income, and cash equivalents.

For a moderate risk profile, with 10 years until retirement, the asset allocation is…

Asset allocation (Table D-1):

Equity:	70%	($70,000)
Fixed income:	30%	($30,000)
Cash Equivalents:	0%	($0)

Step 2 - Determine the asset allocation and investment dollars.

Using Tables D-2 and D-3, find the columns which match the years until retirement and risk tolerance. These columns reveal the percentages for each of the equity (large cap, small/mid cap, and foreign) and fixed income (US Government and corporate bonds) categories.

Equity allocation (Table D-2):

Large Cap:	25%	($25,000)
Small/Mid Cap:	20%	($20,000)
Foreign:	25%	($25,000)

Fixed Income allocation (Table D-3):

US Government	20%	($20,000)
Corporate	10%	($10,000)

Step 3 - Make equity selections.

Make the equity investment selections; i.e., choose which equity funds to purchase. Using Appendix E, Tables E-1, E-2, and E-3, select appropriate investments for each of the equity groups: large cap, small/mid cap, and foreign. For example, in this case, the selections might be:

Large Cap - 25% (Table E-1)

Vanguard 500 Index Fund (VFINX) $25,000

Small/Mid Cap - 20% (Table E-2)

iShares S&P MidCap 400 ETF (IJJ) $20,000

Foreign - 25% (Table E-3)

Vanguard Total Intl. Stock Index Fund

(VGTSX) $25,000

Note: when investing in mutual funds, the order to buy is placed for a specific dollar amount, not the exact number of shares. However, ETFs are bought and sold like a share of stock; the order is placed for a specific number of shares. To determine the number of ETF shares to buy, divide the dollar amount you are investing by the current ETF share price.

For example, if you are buying $20,000 of an ETF which is currently trading at $51.50 a share, you would purchase 388 shares.

Step 4 - Make the fixed income selections.

Make the fixed income investment selections. Using Table E-4 in Appendix E, select appropriate investments for each of the fixed income groups: U. S. Government and corporate. For this case, the selections might be:

U.S. Government - 20% (Table E-4)

Vanguard Inflation-Protected Securities

(VIPSX) $20,000

Corporates - 10% (Table E-4)

Vanguard Total Bond Market Index

(VBMFX) $10,000

Note: when investing in mutual funds, the order to buy is placed for a specific dollar amount, not the exact number of shares. However, ETFs are bought and sold like a share of stock; the order is placed for a specific number of shares. To determine the number of ETF shares to buy, divide the dollar amount you are investing by the current ETF share price.

> For example, if you are buying $15,000 of an ETF which is currently trading at $34.50 a share, you would purchase 434 shares.

Summary:

Case #1 Investment Portfolio - $100,000 Total Portfolio

Vanguard 500 Index Fund (VFINX)	$25,000
iShares S&P MidCap 400 ETF (IJJ)	$20,000
Vanguard Total Intl. Stock Index Fund (VGTSX)	$25,000
Vanguard Inflation-Protected Securities (VIPSX)	$20,000
Vanguard Total Bond Market Index (VBMFX)	$10,000

Case #2

Years until retirement: **3**

Risk tolerance: **Conservative**

Portfolio size: **$300,000**

Step 1 - Select the years until retirement and risk tolerance.

Return to the Asset Allocation Tables in Appendix D, where you determined your asset mix based on your investor profile: risk tolerance, temperament, and years until retirement. On Table D-1, find the columns which match the years until retirement and risk tolerance. The column reveals the percentage allocation for each asset class: equities, fixed income, and cash equivalents.

For a conservative risk profile, with 3 years until retirement, the asset allocation is…

Asset allocation (Table D-1):

Equity:	40%	($120,000)
Fixed income:	55%	($165,000)
Cash Equivalents:	5%	($15,000)

Step 2 - Determine the asset allocation and investment dollars.

Using Tables D-2 and D-3, find the columns which match the years until retirement and risk tolerance. These columns reveal the percentages for each of the equity (large cap, small/mid cap, and foreign) and fixed income (US Government and corporate bonds) categories.

Equity allocation (Table D-2):

Large Cap:	15%	($45,000)
Small/Mid Cap:	10%	($30,000)
Foreign:	15%	($45,000)

Fixed Income allocation (Table D-3):

US Government	35%	($120,000)
Corporate	20%	($45,000)

Step 3 - Make equity selections.

Make the equity investment selections; i.e., choose which equity funds to purchase. Using Appendix E, Tables E-1, E-2, and E-3, select appropriate investments for each of the equity groups: large cap, small/mid cap, and foreign. For example, in this case, the selections might be:

Large Cap - 15% (Table E-1)

Vanguard Large Cap Index ETF (VV) $45,000

Small/Mid Cap - 10% (Table E-2)

Vanguard MidCap Value Index ETF (VOE) $30,000

Foreign - 15% (Table E-3)

Vanguard FTSE All World Ex. US Index ETF (VEU) $45,000

Note: when investing in mutual funds, the order to buy is placed for a specific dollar amount, not the exact number of shares. However, ETFs are bought and sold like a share of stock; the order is placed for a specific number of shares. To determine the number of ETF shares to buy, divide the dollar amount you are investing by the current ETF share price.

> For example, if you are buying $20,000 of an ETF which is currently trading at $51.50 a share, you would purchase 388 shares.

Step 4 - Make the fixed income selections.

Make the fixed income investment selections. Using Table E-4 in Appendix E, select appropriate investments for each of the fixed income groups: U. S. Government and corporate. For this case, the selections might be:

U.S. Government - 35% (Table E-4)

Vanguard Inflation-Protected Securities

(VIPSX) $105,000

Corporates - 20% (Table E-4)

Vanguard Total Bond Market Index

(VBMFX) $60,000

Note: when investing in mutual funds, the order to buy is placed for a specific dollar amount, not the exact number of shares. However, ETFs are bought and sold like a share of stock; the order is placed for a specific number of shares. To determine the number of ETF shares to buy, divide the dollar amount you are investing by the current ETF share price.

> For example, if you are buying $15,000 of an ETF

which is currently trading at $34.50 a share, you would purchase 434 shares.

Summary:

Case #2 Investment Portfolio - $300,000 Total Portfolio

Vanguard Large Cap Index ETF (VV)	$45,000
Vanguard MidCap Value Index ETF (VOE)	$30,000
Vanguard FTSE All World Ex. US Index ETF (VEU)	$45,000
Vanguard Inflation-Protected Securities (VIPSX)	$105,000
Vanguard Total Bond Market Index (VBMFX)	$60,000
Cash equivalents	$15,000

Case #3

Years until retirement: **7**

Risk tolerance: **Aggressive**

Portfolio size: **$600,000**

Step 1 - Select the years until retirement and risk tolerance.

Return to the Asset Allocation Tables in Appendix D, where you determined your asset mix based on your investor profile: risk tolerance, temperament, and years until retirement. On Table D-1, find the columns which match the years until retirement and risk tolerance. The column reveals the percentage allocation for each asset class: equities, fixed income, and cash equivalents.

For an aggressive risk profile, with 7 years until retirement, the asset allocation is…

Asset allocation (Table D-1):

Equity:	75%	($450,000)
Fixed income:	25%	($150,000)
Cash Equivalents:	0%	($0)

Step 2 - Determine the asset allocation and investment dollars.

Using Tables D-2 and D-3, find the columns which match the years until retirement and risk tolerance. These columns reveal the percentages for each of the equity (large cap, small/mid cap, and foreign) and fixed income (US Government and corporate bonds) categories.

Equity allocation (Table D-2):

Large Cap:	20%	($120,000)
Small/Mid Cap:	35%	($210,000)
Foreign:	20%	($120,000)

Fixed Income allocation (Table D-3):

US Government	10%	($60,000)
Corporate	15%	($90,000)

Step 3 - Make equity selections.

Make the equity investment selections; i.e., choose which equity funds to purchase. Using Appendix E, Tables E-1, E-2, and E-3, select appropriate investments for each of the equity groups: large cap, small/mid cap, and foreign. For example, in this case, the selections might be:

Large Cap - 20% (Table E-1)
- Vanguard Large Cap Index ETF (VV) — $120,000

Small/Mid Cap - 35% (Table E-2)
- Vanguard Small Cap Index ETF (VB) — $105,000
- Janus Mid Cap Value (JMCVX) — $105,000

Foreign - 20% (Table E-3)
- iShares MSCI Emerging Markets Index (EEM) — $60,000

Vanguard FTSE All World Ex. US
Index ETF (VEU) $60,000

Note: when investing in mutual funds, the order to buy is placed for a specific dollar amount, not the exact number of shares. However, ETFs are bought and sold like a share of stock; the order is placed for a specific number of shares. To determine the number of ETF shares to buy, divide the dollar amount you are investing by the current ETF share price.

> For example, if you are buying $20,000 of an ETF which is currently trading at $51.50 a share, you would purchase 388 shares.

Step 4 - Make the fixed income selections.

Make the fixed income investment selections. Using Table E-4 in Appendix E, select appropriate investments for each of the fixed income groups: U. S. Government and corporate. For this case, the selections might be:

U.S. Government - 10% (Table E-4)
iShares Barclays TIPS Bond (TIP) $60,000
Corporates - 15% (Table E-4)
Vanguard Total Bond Market
Index (VBMFX) $90,000

Note: when investing in mutual funds, the order to buy is placed for a specific dollar amount, not the exact number of shares. However, ETFs are bought and sold like a share of stock; the order is placed for a specific number of shares. To determine the number of ETF shares to buy, divide the dollar amount you are investing by the current ETF share price.

> For example, if you are buying $15,000 of an ETF which is currently trading at $34.50 a share, you would purchase 434 shares.

Summary:

Case #3 Investment Portfolio - $600,000 Total Portfolio

Vanguard Large Cap Index ETF (VV)	$120,000
Vanguard Small Cap Index ETF (VB)	$105,000
Janus Mid Cap Value (JMCVX)	$105,000
iShares MSCI Emerging Markets Index (EEM)	$60,000
Vanguard FTSE All World Ex. US Index ETF (VEU)	$60,000
iShares Barclays TIPS Bond (TIP)	$60,000
Vanguard Total Bond Market Index (VBMFX)	$90,000

Case #4

Years until retirement: **0** (in retirement)

Risk tolerance: **Moderate**

Portfolio size: **$300,000**

Step 1 - Select the years until retirement and risk tolerance.

Return to the Asset Allocation Tables in Appendix D, where you determined your asset mix based on your investor profile: risk tolerance, temperament, and years until retirement. On Table D-1, find the column you have selected as the best fit for your asset mix of equities, fixed income, and cash equivalents.

For a moderate risk profile, in retirement, the asset allocation is...

Asset allocation (Table D-1):

Equity:	40%	($120,000)
Fixed income:	55%	($165,000)
Cash Equivalents:	5%	($15,000)

Step 2 - Determine the asset allocation and investment dollars.

Using Tables D-2 and D-3, find the columns which match the years until retirement and risk tolerance. These columns reveal the percentages for each of the equity (large cap, small/mid cap, and foreign) and fixed income (U.S. Government and corporate bonds) categories.

Equity allocation (Table D-2):

Large Cap:	15%	($45,000)
Small/Mid Cap:	10%	($30,000)
Foreign:	15%	($45,000)

Fixed Income allocation (Table D-3):

U.S. Government	35%	($105,000)
Corporate	20%	($60,000)

Step 3 - Make equity selections.

Make your equity investment selections. Using Appendix E, Tables E-1, E-2, and E-3, select appropriate investments for each of the equity groups: large cap, small/mid cap, and foreign. For example, in this case, the selections might be:

Large Cap - 15% (Table E-1)
Vanguard Large Cap Index ETF
(V V) $45,000
Small/Mid Cap - 15% (Table E-2)
Vanguard Mid Cap Value
Index ETF (VOE) $30,000
Foreign - 15% (Table E-3)
Vanguard FTSE All World
Ex. US Index ETF (VEU) $45,000

Note: when investing in mutual funds, the order is placed for a specific dollar amount, not the exact number of shares. However, ETFs are bought and sold like a share of stock, so the order is placed for a specific number of shares. To determine the number of ETF shares to buy, divide the dollar amount you are investing by the current ETF share price.

For example, if you are buying $20,000 of an ETF which is currently trading at $34.50 a share, you would purchase 579 shares.

Step 4 - Make the fixed income selections.

Make your fixed income investment selections. Using Table E-4 in Appendix E, select appropriate investments for each of the fixed income groups: U. S. Government and corporate. For this case, the selections might be:

U.S. Government - 35% (Table E-4)
Vanguard Inflation-Protected Securities
(VIPSX) $105,000
Corporates - 20% (Table E-4)
Vanguard Int. Term Bond Index
(VBIIX) $60,000

Note: when investing in mutual funds, the order is placed for a specific dollar amount, not the exact number of shares. However, ETFs are bought and sold like a share of stock, so the order is placed for a specific number of shares. To determine the number of ETF shares to buy, divide the dollar amount you are investing by the current ETF share price.

For example, if you are buying $15,000 of an ETF which is

currently trading at $34.50 a share, you would purchase 434 shares.

Summary:

Case #4 Investment Portfolio - $300,000 Total Portfolio

Vanguard Large Cap Index ETF (VV)	$45,000
Vanguard Mid Cap Value Index ETF (VOE)	$30,000
Vanguard FTSE All World Ex. US Index ETF (VEU)	$45,000
Vanguard Inflation-Protected Securities (VIPSX)	$105,000
Vanguard Int. Term Bond Index (VBIIX)	$60,000
Cash equivalents	$15,000

The previous case examples demonstrated the procedure for making your personal investment selections using asset allocations.

Making Your Investment Selections

Now select the investments which match your personal investment profile. Turn to Table D-4 in Appendix D for a worksheet where you will make a list of each investment with the percentages and dollar amounts that match your particular profile and total portfolio amount.

Step 1. On table D-1, locate the column which matched your years until retirement and risk tolerance.

From Table D-1, fill in the following asset allocation for your profile:

Equities: __________%
Fixed Income: __________%
Cash Equivalents: __________%

Step 2. Using Tables D-2 and D-3, find the columns which match your profile and fill in the following:

Equity (Table D-2)
Large Cap: __________%
Small/Mid Cap __________%
Foreign: __________%

Fixed Income (Table D-3)
U.S. Government __________%
Corporates __________%

Transfer the percentages above to the Percentage column on the appropriate rows on Table D-4.

Calculate the dollar amount you will invest for each investment category. The dollar amount for each investment category is your total portfolio amount multiplied by the percentage for that category. For example, if your total portfolio is $400,000 and the Large Cap percentage is 15%, the amount to invest in that category is ($400,000 x .15) $60,000. Record these amounts in the Amount Invested column of Table D-4, for each category.

Step 3. Using Tables E-1, E-2 and E-3, choose the **equity** mutual funds or ETFs for purchase in each category. Regardless of your risk tolerance and years until retirement, you should make a selection for each of the three equity categories: Large Cap, Small/Mid Cap, and Foreign equities. Write the names and symbols of these selections in the Investment Selected and Symbol columns of Table D-4.

Step 4. Using Table E-4, choose the **fixed income** mutual funds or ETFs for purchase in each of the categories. Depending upon your risk tolerance and years until retirement, you may or may not have an amount to invest in fixed income. Write the names and symbols of these selections, if any, in the Investment Selected and Symbol columns of Table D-4.

You've done it! That wasn't so bad was it? Think about what you've accomplished:

- Determined your investment profile - risk tolerance.
- Estimated the number of years until you retire.
- Established an Asset Allocation for your total investment portfolio which is appropriate to your situation, tolerance, and goals.
- Set percentages for each investment class/category.
- Determined a dollar amount to invest in each category.
- Selected mutual funds and ETFs in those investment categories.

Chapter 11 will show you how to open investment accounts and place orders for these investments.

As you have just learned, selecting investments is not rocket science even though some people try to make it seem like that. Today, investors have thousands of investment choices which were not available to previous generations. Using low cost mutual funds and ETFs, along with discernment and annual reviews, you can have a well-balanced portfolio which will generate income for your retirement years.

By discernment, I mean evaluating the funds you use with respect to performance and reasonable expenses. The funds I have mentioned in this book all have expense ratios under 1%. They also have better than average long-term performance, they beat the index that measures the performance in their category, or they are structured to hold the same investments as the indices. Be sure to keep up to date on your selections through independent rankings such as Morningstar or Lipper. Also visit www.InvestorTrainer.com to see a current list of mutual funds and ETFs which meet the criteria I have used in this book: performance and expense ratios.

Chapter Questions

1. What financial assets are included when calculating your Total Portfolio?
2. What are the three major asset classes used to create your asset allocation?
3. Why might it be wise to include inflation-protected bonds in your portfolio?

Chapter 10
Model Portfolios

Chapter Objectives

- See emotional reactions to others' successes.
- Understand the purpose of three model portfolios.
- Recognize the appropriateness of the Hound Dog Portfolio.
- Recognize the usefulness of the Retiree Portfolio.
- Recognize the purpose of the Insured Portfolio.
- See the role of inflation-protected investments in a portfolio.

Why Consider a Model Portfolio?

Have you ever been at a social event or standing around the office water cooler as someone pontificates about the 'killing' they made in a stock or other investment? It seems their selection and timing was near perfection. We think what brilliance and foresight they must have to be able to make such an outstanding, *can't-go-wrong* investment. The temptation to want to sit at their feet and absorb their strategy for successful investing can sometimes be overwhelming.

But before you fall at their feet, remember that most of us like to share stories of our successes. It makes us feel good. And there is nothing wrong with that when it's appropriate and we work in some degree of humility. But keep in mind that most of us do not like to stand around and tell others of the mistakes we made along the way. That doesn't feel good.

These contrasting feelings are basic human emotions that are wired in to all of us. And just as basic to investing is an understanding that not all investments are appropriate for your situation or will make you money. Choosing an appropriate investment is one of the most important decisions that an investor will make.

So what is the investor to do? How does he or she go about selecting investments that balance risk and reward and are appropriate for his or her situation?

For starters, you could educate yourself on the basics of investing and apply that understanding to the advice you will no doubt receive from numerous sources. For relief from insomnia, you could dig through research reports and economic projections.

Or you might follow the method outlined in the previous chapter and select from a list of appropriate funds which fit your investing objectives. This is my recommended approach and the one that I teach investors to follow as I help them make investment selections.

However, it's not easy for everyone to select investments, even mutual funds and ETFs. Many people do not have the financial background, investing experience, or interest in investing to make investment selections with confidence. And confidence is essential if we are going to stick with our investment plan in up markets, down markets, and tsunamis.

I wrote this book to help non-professional investors understand what is involved in planning and *investing for retirement* and to offer specific investment suggestions that will fit their particular investing profile. If you have made any attempt to educate yourself and read retirement planning literature, you no doubt have run across other writers offering suggestions for structuring an investment portfolio. Most of the suggested portfolios use index mutual funds and ETFs as the investments. That is a proven, time-tested investment structure and it's also the one I'm suggesting you implement for your investing plan.

Most people, regardless of age, will find it easier and more appropriate to use index mutual funds or ETFs than individual stocks in their investment portfolio. And some investors will go through the process of determining an appropriate asset allocation only to become confused or intimidated by the investment selection process.

Therefore, for those of you who are unsure, uncomfortable, or otherwise unable to make investment selections, I recommend that you use one of the model portfolios presented in this chapter. I have given each portfolio a name to set it apart and help identify its comfort level.

I call the first portfolio the **Hound Dog Portfolio**. It will best fit investors who are still working and *investing for retirement* and want steady growth. I named this portfolio in honor of my Basset Hound, Rocket. She was loyal, lovable, and always there. The Hound Dog Portfolio offers an allocation for investors seeking moderate, year after year, steady asset growth.

The second portfolio I call the **Retiree Portfolio.** As its name implies, it's for those now living off their investments and savings. This portfolio offers income, with preservation of assets, and the opportunity for modest growth. It's a conservative allocation for retirees who cannot assume significant stock market risks but recognize a need to keep some of their assets invested in equities in order to keep up with inflation.

The third portfolio I have named the **Insured Portfolio** . This portfolio is also for retirees but has an even more risk-averse allocation. It's tuned for people who can't sleep at night knowing that their stocks or mutual funds may have fluctuated during the day.

The Hound Dog Portfolio

The Hound Dog Portfolio is for investors with a long-term perspective, who are seeking moderate growth of their assets and are willing to assume a moderate level of risk. This portfolio is oriented toward growth using equities, with a degree of asset stability from fixed income investments.

The Hound Dog Portfolio does not allocate cash equivalents, since investor temperaments will differ, and the cash portion of your portfolio may be anywhere from 0% to 20%, depending upon your risk tolerance and temperament. Therefore these percentages represent only the investment (equity and fixed income), non-cash portion of your portfolio. As I have previously mentioned, the best investments for helping investors achieve their goals are index mutual funds and ETFs.

Hound Dog Portfolio

Investment	Symbol	Portfolio Percentage
Vanguard Large Cap Index ETF	VV	25
Vanguard MidCap Value Index ETF	VOE	15
Vanguard Total International Stock Index Fund	VGTSX	20
Vanguard Inflation-Protected Securities Fund	VIPSX	40

Hound Dog Portfolio Details:

Vanguard Large Cap Index ETF: tracks a large-capitalization stock index, in the large blend category; expense ratio is .07%. This ETF trades on the New York Stock Exchange.
Rationale: growth; using large, established U.S. companies.

Vanguard MidCap Value Index ETF: tracks a mid-capitalization stock index with wider price fluctuation than the large-cap index; in the mid-capitalization value category; expense ratio is .13%. This ETF trades on the New York Stock Exchange.
Rationale: growth; using mid and small capitalization U.S. companies.

Vanguard Total International Stock Index Fund: International Global stock index, in the foreign large blend category; expense ratio is .27%; may be purchased directly from Vanguard or through a broker.
Rationale: growth; exposure to international companies and economies.

Vanguard Inflation-Protected Securities Fund: Inflation-indexed U.S. Treasury and government agency bonds; in the inflation-protected bond category; expense ratio is .20%; may be purchased directly from Vanguard or through a broker.
Rationale: portfolio stability and income; protection from rise in rate of inflation.

The Retiree Portfolio

The Retiree Portfolio is best suited for retirees who primarily need income but want modest growth of their assets to help keep up with inflation. The priority is on income, then preservation of assets with some growth.

Cash equivalents are an important financial component for retirees and are therefore included in this portfolio. Keep a minimum balance of three months' living expenses in a money market account and the balance of your cash in short-term CDs with maturities ranging from 3 to 12 months, depending upon your comfort level.

Notice in this portfolio that all the investments are mutual funds except the Vanguard MidCap Value Index ETF. This is to make it easier to arrange for periodic distributions from the funds.

Retirees need income, and a direct deposit monthly or quarterly into a checking or savings account can be easily arranged. Mutual fund companies usually offer this service to investors at no additional cost. Check with the mutual fund, as there may be minimum fund balance requirements for this service.

Retiree Portfolio

Investment	Symbol	Portfolio Percentage
Vanguard 500 Index Fund	VFINX	15
Vanguard MidCap Value Index ETF	VOE	5
Vanguard Total International Stock Index Fund	VGTSX	10
Vanguard Inflation-Protected Securities Fund	VIPSX	60
Cash Equivalents		10

Retiree Portfolio Details:

Vanguard 500 Index Fund: US large-capitalization stock fund which tracks the S&P 500 Index; expense ratio is .15%; may be purchased directly from Vanguard or through a broker.
Rationale: growth; using large, established U.S. companies.

Vanguard MidCap Value Index ETF: tracks a mid-capitalization stock index with wider fluctuation than the large-cap index, in the mid-capitalization value category; expense ratio is .13%. This ETF trades on the New York Stock Exchange.
Rationale: growth; using mid and small capitalization U.S. companies.

Vanguard Total International Stock Index Fund: International Global stock index, in the foreign large blend category; expense ratio is .27%; may be purchased directly from Vanguard or through a broker.
Rationale: growth; exposure to international companies and economies.

Vanguard Inflation-Protected Securities Fund: Inflation-indexed U.S. Treasury and government agency bonds; in the inflation-protected bond category; expense ratio is .20%; may be purchased directly from Vanguard or through a broker.
Rationale: portfolio stability and income; protection from rise in rate of inflation.

Cash Equivalents: a mix of a money market account and a ladder of short-term CDs. The CD maturities should range from 3 to 12 months, depending upon your comfort level. The ladder refers to a series of CDs maturing every month. See the definition of a CD Ladder in the Glossary.
Rationale: safety of principal with income reflecting current short-term CD rates; and some protection from inflation.

The Insured Portfolio

Finally, I offer a portfolio for non-investors—people who can't sleep knowing that their financial assets might fluctuate. This portfolio uses a combination of federally insured certificates of deposit and U.S. Government I-Bonds (Savings Bonds). The appeal of this portfolio is that the principal will not fluctuate; the principal will not decline in absolute dollar terms. The risk in this portfolio is the increased potential for loss of purchasing power of those dollars due to inflation.

The I-Bonds are U.S. Government savings bonds with an inflation kicker. The principal value of the I-Bonds will not fluctuate. The interest rate is reset every six months to reflect the change in the Consumer Price Index; i.e., the interest rate will rise and fall with inflation. The interest earned is not paid out but accumulates in the bond. It is tax-deferred until the bond is cashed in.

This is an excellent investment for risk-averse individuals and those seeking a safe, inflation-protected investment for a portion of their fixed income assets. During periods of negative consumer-price inflation, such as we saw in 2009, these bonds may not pay any interest. This is because the formula used to calculate the bonds' current six month interest rate factors in the most recent consumer-price inflation or deflation. However, the rate is never negative, so the accumulated principal will not decline during deflationary periods. In 2008, the Treasury Department reduced the amount which can be invested in I-Bonds to $10,000 per year per individual using a combination of paper and electronic bonds. These are best used for longer term investments, since there is a one-year minimum holding period and a 90-days-of-interest penalty if cashed in before five years. See I-Bonds in Glossary for more details.

The certificate of deposit portion of the Insured Portfolio should be invested in a ladder of CDs. This ladder will provide a self-renewing series of CDs that mature every three or six months, depending upon your preference. Utilizing a ladder of CDs helps keep your CD portfolio earning an average of current rates, eliminating the possibility of renewing your total CD amount at a low rate just as rates start to rise. See CD Ladder in Glossary, for more details.

Insured Portfolio

Investment	**Portfolio Percentage**
Certificates of Deposit Ladder:	
6-Month CD	15
12-Month CD	15
18-Month CD	15
24-Month CD	15
30-Month CD	15
36-Month CD	15
I-Bonds	10

Note: since the shortest CD maturity in the Insured Portfolio is six months, it's important to have set aside, apart from this portfolio, at least six months of living expenses in money market, savings, or checking accounts.

The Insured Portfolio details:

Certificates of Deposit: a series of 6- to 36-month maturity CDs. The yield will reflect the average CD yield in the series (ladder) as renewal rates fluctuate.

Rationale: absolute safety of principal with income reflecting current CD rates.

I-Bonds: U.S. Savings Bonds with inflation protection. Rates adjust every 6 months to reflect inflation (CPI). Tax-deferred up to 30 years. Minimum holding period one year.
Rationale: absolute safety of principal with protection against inflation; helps reduce interest rate risk.

If you are able to roll over the CD principal at each maturity, not needing to consume principal for expenses, I recommend you increase the amount in I-Bonds up to a level of 20 to 25% of your portfolio. To do this, take out an equal amount from the CD at each maturity and purchase an I-Bond for that amount, not to exceed the maximum permitted by the Treasury Department during any one year.

> For example, in a $100,000 portfolio with $90,000 in CDs and $10,000 in I-Bonds, $15,000 in CDs will mature every six months. At each maturity, roll over $13,500 into a new 36-month CD and purchase $1,500 in I-Bonds. At the end of 36 months, the portfolio will hold $81,000 in CDs and $19,000 in I-Bonds.

Did you notice in these portfolios that the fixed income portion uses an inflation-protected mutual fund or the inflation-protected I-Bond? I've included these inflation-protected investments to protect your portfolio against a rise in inflation and interest rates—a killer of fixed income investments like bonds. When interest rates rise, fixed income investments such as bonds lose market value because their fixed interest payments become less valuable as new bonds with higher interest rates are issued.

> Note: in the post-2008/2009 Crash environment, the U.S. Government has flooded the economy with money. Although politicians seem unable to agree on what to call it, they have agreed to spend taxpayer money to fund it. But regardless of what it is called—bailout, tax-cut, stimulus, TARP, quantitative easing, or rescue—the result is the same: the country is awash in cash, credit stimulus, and government guarantees. And unless the Federal Reserve and the Obama Administration are very skilled and fortunate, this cash infusion will lead to increased inflation in the next few years.

I offer these three model portfolios as alternatives for those of you who find selecting your own investments to be a daunting task. They offer a track record, diversification, and an asset allocation appropriate to your situation and risk tolerance. Remember, whether you choose one of these portfolios or follow the guidance from Chapter 9, be sure your risk tolerance is accommodated. If you are not comfortable with your investment plan, you are more likely to become fearful during economic turbulence and make strategic investing mistakes.

Chapter Questions

1. What is the objective of the Hound Dog Portfolio?

2. What is the objective of the Retiree Portfolio?

3. What is the objective of the Insured Portfolio?

4. Which portfolio comes closer to meeting your investment objectives? Why?

5. Describe the purpose and structure of a CD ladder.

6. List several features of I-Bonds. What investment objective do they fulfill?

Chapter 11
Implementing Your Investment Plan

Chapter Objectives

- Understand your implementation choices.
- Realize the difference between full service and discount brokers.
- Know the different account choices and purposes.
- Know the steps to opening an account.
- Understand how to place an order.
- Understand the advantage of using dollar cost averaging.

Now that you have set your asset allocation and selected your investments, it's time to understand how you deal with an investment firm, open an account, and make the investment purchase. For the novice or first time investor this may seem like a daunting task. You know the mutual fund you want to purchase, but how do you buy it?

Regulatory Protections

Fortunately, we can't buy securities off the street or at a garage sale. Financial securities are purchased through a licensed broker at a registered investment firm. In case you think this may be a disadvantage—some sort of conspiracy designed to take more money from investors— consider the alternative. How do you know you are getting what you were told you were buying, or thought you were purchasing? Was the price you paid correct?

The integrity of the salesperson and the investment firm that you are dealing with is critical to the delivery of the item you purchased, whether it be a vehicle, big screen TV, or shares of a mutual fund.

The trust factor in the financial markets is enormous. It is the grease that keeps financial markets functioning smoothly. However, this trust causes investors, brokers, and financial markets to assume responsibility for understanding the consequence of and honoring their commitments and decisions.

Do you remember the expression, *Caveat Emptor - let the buyer beware*? A modern day investing twist of this warning is, know who you are investing with and understand what you are buying.

How important is this? Recall the events of December 2008, and the name Bernard Madoff. Mr. Madoff pled guilty to fraud charges involving what may be the largest Ponzi scheme in history, defrauding his clients out of possibly $65 billion. The long-term return on the investments of his victims was extraordinary—very stable and above average in both up and down markets. When his victims were asked how could you have fallen for his scam, one victim replied, "We thought we had hit the lottery... we didn't ask questions." Many of his clients later said they did not understand how he could achieve these generous returns or what their money was invested in; they only knew they were getting an above average return, so why question his methods?

Maybe you think this is an isolated example. Or maybe only people willing to gamble with their finances for oversized gains might fall for such schemes. Let me remind you of another headline a few months after Mr. Madoff's unraveling. In February 2009, the Stanford Financial Group was shut down by regulators who alleged "a fraudulent, multi-billion dollar investment scheme."[17]

It seems Stanford Financial, through its off-shore bank, was offering "investment opportunities that sounded almost too good to be true: promises of lucrative returns on relatively safe certificates of deposit that were often more than twice the going rate offered by mainstream banks."[18] Yes, even CD savers can get caught up in these schemes.

If this attitude surprises you, re-read Rule One - Know Yourself. When it comes to our investments, our emotions will swing between fear and greed. Only when we can catch ourselves and recognize that these emotions are kicking in, will we be able to use sound judgment in our financial decisions.

The securities laws in the United States are in place to protect the investor from misrepresentation, fraud, and unscrupulous sales people. During the Great Depression of the 1930's a number of investor protections were implemented. The Securities Act of 1933 (issuance and registration of securities), The Securities Exchange Act of 1934 (sale of securities, brokerage firms and exchanges), the Investment Company Act of 1940 (mutual funds), and the Investment Adviser's Act of 1940 are just a few examples of laws regulating the creation, sale, and promotion of investments to the public. Later amendments and other laws are also designed for our protection.

The bottom line for all investors is that we must transact our investment purchases with a registered representative (salesperson) at a registered investment firm and understand what we are buying.

These investment firms are licensed to sell securities and therefore fall under the law and the scrutiny of security regulators. That provides us the protection and provision for redress if we are fraudulently treated in our investing pursuits. But it does not eliminate the responsibility we have to understand what we are investing in and with whom we are investing.

We can seek redress if someone fraudulently misrepresents an investment that we purchase or commits a security law violation against us. We are not protected against our mistakes in judgment or selection of investments. Again, be sure you are familiar with Rule One.

Fortunately, there are several watchdog groups, formed by the securities laws previously mentioned, and independent regulators which provide information about licensed investment professionals and firms. You can check out brokers and investment firms at various web sites, including…

- FINRA (Financial Industry Regulatory Authority) www.finra.org/Investors/index.htm
- BrokerCheck (is the broker licensed?) www.finra.org/brokercheck/
- Investor Alerts www.finra.org/Investors/ProtectYourself/InvestorAlerts/index.htm
- Securities Investor Protection Corporation (is the firm a member?) www.sipc.org/who/database.cfm

If you are contacted by a salesperson or organization, and *you did not initiate the contact*, be careful. It is critical that you do your homework and check out both the firm and salesperson.

Account Choices

In prior generations our parents did their banking with a bank and investing with a traditional brokerage firm. Today, investors may conduct financial transactions with many different investment sales organizations. We may purchase investments and conduct our banking with a traditional brokerage firm, discount broker, bank, credit union, or directly from a mutual fund company. With minor exceptions, they all can sell us essentially the same investment products: stocks, bonds, mutual funds, ETFs, even checking accounts and CDs.

So how do you decide whom to use? My advice is to make the selection of the brokerage firm on the basis of trust and reputation; standing with the regulatory organizations; how easy they are to contact; and how available someone is to answer your questions, concerns, and to take your orders. For some of you this may mean staying with the broker with whom you already have a relationship. For others it may mean selecting a national discount brokerage, one that provides easy access via a toll-free number and Internet web site.

Keep in mind that the more handholding you need after the account is opened, the more likely you are to need a full service brokerage firm. Discount brokers usually don't provide individualized handholding past a few basic services, such as opening an account and giving you a call or email a few times a year to see if you might need to make additional investments or IRA contributions. Full service brokers will provide the services you need to open the account and advise you concerning which investments to purchase. Their service and attention can be helpful, but their commissions and charges can be considerably higher than a discount broker.

I prefer the discount brokerage route. Discount brokers provide the same investment choices but with a much smaller transaction fee or commission. With a discount broker, you will have to make your own investment decisions. I have seen some full service commissions run up past $600 for the same purchase (or sale) of stock that a discount brokerage might charge $9 to process. Ask any brokerage firm that you are considering for a schedule of the commissions and account fees before opening the account.

Don't let making an investment decision intimidate you. Using this book, the web site www.InvestorTrainer.com, investment advisory services and other authors, you can make informed decisions regarding your investment choices. The more you learn about investing and the long-term track record of various asset classes of investments, the more confidence you will have in your investment selections. And the more confidence you have in your decisions, the more likely you will be to stick with your investment plan.

The following is an incomplete list of investment brokerage firms by firm type:

- Traditional full service brokerage firms:
  Merrill Lynch; Edward Jones; Raymond James
- Discount brokerage firms:
  Charles Schwab, TD Ameritrade, Fidelity, Scottrade, E*Trade, USAA
- Mutual fund companies:
  Fidelity Investments, Vanguard, USAA, T. Rowe Price
- Banks, credit unions:
  most have registered representatives on staff or affiliated.

I could have generated several pages of investment firms which offer brokerage services. The list above is neither complete nor a recommendation. It's only an example of the choices you have to choose from. Any one of those firms can provide you all the investment and banking services you may need.

You should make the choice of investment firm on the basis of trust, reputation, and service, not on the basis of the lowest commission for a stock trade or mutual fund purchase. It's a mistake to purchase an ETF for a $5 commission, ignoring the firm which charges $9 or more, if the firm you selected doesn't provide proper servicing of your account or easy access to someone who can fix mistakes.

Types of Accounts

Investing accounts can be broken into three general groups:

- Taxable accounts - taxes are paid each year.
- Retirement accounts - taxes are deferred.
- Banking accounts - holds savings and cash for current needs.

The difference between the taxable account and the retirement account is the tax treatment. Taxes are paid each year on the taxable account, whereas the taxes are deferred on retirement accounts until you withdraw money from the account. Both types of account can hold the same variety of investments: stocks, bonds, mutual funds, ETFs, money market account, CDs. Banking accounts are the traditional checking and savings accounts. These accounts are convenient for money needed on a short-term basis, like paying bills. Additionally, these accounts are where you should keep your six-month emergency savings.

Taxable accounts

These are broad, all inclusive accounts which may hold almost any investment offered to investors: stocks, bonds, mutual funds, ETFs, commodities, real estate, CDs, etc. The earnings and capital gains from the sale of investments are taxed in the current year. Losses from the sale of an investment may be deducted from your current year taxes up to $3,000, with amounts above $3,000 carried over to future years.

Retirement accounts

These accounts are divided into two groups: tax-deferred and tax-free.

- Tax-deferred account - such as traditional IRA and 401(k) accounts. Taxes are not due until the year you withdraw funds. For tax purposes, all withdrawals are treated as ordinary income. Retirement accounts may hold any IRS approved investment, such as stocks, bonds, mutual funds, ETFs, most publicly traded investments, and CDs. The IRS does not allow investments such as collectibles or direct ownership of real estate to be held in an Individual Retirement Account.

- Tax-free account - such as a Roth IRA or Roth 401(k). The income and capital gains from the investments are not taxed, now or in the future, when you withdraw funds after age 59½ and the account has been open for at least 5years.

The investments in retirement accounts are held by a custodial firm. The IRA custodian could be a brokerage firm, mutual fund company, or bank, in addition to others. Some savers mistakenly assume if you have an IRA, it must be with a bank and must be invested in a CD. This is not true. Today, brokerage firms and mutual fund companies offer a full line of investments, including CDs, and banks offer a full line of investments along with CDs.

There are limitations on IRA eligibility, deductibility of contributions from your taxes, and contribution levels. In 2011, eligible investors may make IRA contributions up to $5,000, and those 50 or older may contribute an additional $1,000. These contribution levels are subject to change as Congress sees fit.

The great advantage of retirement accounts is the tax deferral. No tax is due on the earnings from the investments until you make withdrawals from the account. The earnings and capital gains remain in the account with no reduction for taxes. The IRS does require that you begin taking withdrawals, called the Minimum Required Distribution (MRD), from these retirement accounts when you reach 70½. The annual MRD is calculated using your life expectancy and the value of the retirement account on December 31 of the previous year.

The Roth IRA is the best retirement account yet devised. It is tax-free, not merely tax-deferred. The Roth IRA does not require any withdrawal, regardless of your age. There are income limitations on who may contribute to a Roth IRA, and it must be opened a minimum of five years before you can withdraw tax-free. The next two chapters present more detail on Individual Retirement Accounts and employer-sponsored retirement plans.

Summary of Types of Accounts

Investment Company	What Investments	Taxes
Taxable Investment Accounts		
Brokerage firms Mutual fund companies Banks Credit unions	mutual funds, ETFs, stocks, bonds, CDs, money market accounts,	Due in current year
Retirement Accounts: Traditional IRA, 401(k), 403(b), SEP IRA		
Brokerage firms Mutual fund companies Banks Credit unions	mutual funds, ETFs, stocks, bonds, CDs, money market accounts	Tax-deferred until withdrawn
Retirement Accounts: Roth IRA, Roth 401(k), Roth 403(b)		
Brokerage firms Mutual fund companies Banks Credit unions	mutual funds, ETFs, stocks, bonds, CDs, money market accounts	Tax-free

Summary of Selected Retirement Accounts

Account type	Taxes	Contribution Limits[a]; Income Restrictions to Participate; Deductibility from Taxes	With-drawal Require-ment by
Tradi-tional IRA	Tax-deferred	Contribution limits: smaller of - $5,000, $6,000 (age 50 years +), or 100% of earnings. Income restriction: none Deductible: AGI[1]	First year after you reach 70½
Roth IRA	Tax-free	Contribution limits: smaller of - $5,000, $6,000 (50 years +), or 100% of earnings. Income restriction: AGI[2] Joint: $179,000 Single: $122,000 Deductible: No	None
401(k) 403(b)	Tax-deferred	Contribution limits: smaller of – $15,500, $20,500 (50 years +), or 100% of earnings. Indexed to inflation; ask plan administrator for specifics Income restrictions: none Deductibility: income deferral	First year after you reach 70½
Roth 401(k) Roth 403(b)	Tax-free	Contribution limits: smaller of – $15,500, $20,500 (50 years +), or 100% of earnings. Indexed to inflation; ask plan administrator for specifics Income restrictions: none Deductibility: none	First year after you reach 70½

Notes: see next page.

[1] AGI - Adjusted Gross Income restrictions.
[2] AGI - Adjusted Gross Income maximum phase out of eligibility to make contribution.
[a] Contribution limits are generally indexed to inflation and will increase in the future.

Opening an Account

Now, armed with an understanding of the types of investment accounts available and the choices of firms with which to do your investing—brokerage firms, mutual fund companies, and banks—it's time to step out and open an account or two. After opening a retirement account, you should next consider opening a taxable investment account as soon as you can financially swing it.

Don't let the thought of opening an investment account intimidate you. The investment firms want your business. Remember, they do not make money without your business; you are their customer.

Steps for opening an investment account:

1. Select an investment firm. This is your call—discount broker, full service broker, or mutual fund company. Check the regulatory agencies for the status of their registration and any possible unresolved complaints. Talk to several firms; get a feel for ease of access to someone who can answer your questions.
2. Call the securities firm directly on their toll-free number and tell them you want to open an account. Ask for the fee and commission schedules in addition to the new account

form. If you have decided to open both a taxable account and an IRA, let them know at this time. Each account requires a separate form.

3. If you have accounts already established (taxable or retirement) with another firm, and you want to consolidate these into one account, let the representative you are speaking with know this also. You may consolidate either taxable accounts or retirement accounts. The brokerage firm will handle all the details of transferring the investments and monies from the other firm. You will not need to contact the firm you are leaving.
4. Complete the new account form and return it to the selected investment company. Include a check for the opening deposit, unless you are transferring an existing account. Call the toll-free number for assistance if needed. This call will also give you insight into the quality of their service. You will never again be more important than at this time as a new customer.
5. Once the account is opened and funded, or securities and monies have been transferred in, you are ready to contact the investment firm and place your order for the investments which you have selected.

Placing an Order

First-time investors may be intimidated when thinking about calling in an order to purchase a stock or mutual fund. Trust me; it can be a pleasant straightforward experience. It is easier and less stressful than ordering a sandwich at a New York City deli during the lunch hour.

> During my training with Merrill Lynch in New York, I had an hour for lunch most days. After a few days of eating at a lunchroom in the building, I was ready to venture out and experience what New York City had to offer during the lunch hour rush.
>
> I asked one of the locals for a recommendation for a good, quick, cheap place to grab a sandwich and still be able to get back within the hour. In 1983, cheap was important, as I was living on $15 a day for all my living expenses except lodging. She recommended a great little deli around the corner and gave me some advice: "Do not look the guy behind the counter in the eye until you know what you want to order!" That was great advice.
>
> As I left the building, I could not help but notice that people were everywhere. The sidewalks were crowded as workers did the New York sprint to get errands run and to grab a quick lunch. The place she recommended was packed almost to the door with people pushing toward the counter in no particular order or line. Tony, the order-taker would yell out, "Next," fix a stare on someone along the front row, and take the order. It seemed the average

order took less than five seconds to verbalize, be received, written down, and passed on to the sandwich makers. The process went fairly smoothly, and hundreds of customers could be served in the short lunchtime window.

Everything went smoothly, that is, unless you paused in the only part of the process in which you were required to participate: placing the order. There was no tolerance for deviating from the established rules for placing your order. If you inadvertently used a conjunction while verbalizing your order, the order might be rejected, and your place in the order queue ignored. It was not good form to pause or use words like *and*, *or*, or *what*.

Once you got to the counter and had your order clearly in mind, you were expected to look Tony in the eye. When he made eye contact with you, you spoke your order, "Turkey on wheat, mayo, spicy mustard, dressed no pickles." That was it. No further interaction was necessary. If you ordered something that was not available, no problem, you would get a substitute.

This deli became one of my favorite places. I not only enjoyed the great sandwiches but looked forward to the daily joust with the customers and Tony. On the day I got my order placed in just over three seconds, I got a smile from Tony. I had been accepted. I was one of the regulars.

So relax; placing a stock or mutual fund order is not anything like ordering in a New York deli! The process is straightforward, and the order-taker will lead you through the procedure with a series of questions. For your part in the process, you will need to know…

- Your account number.
- Other personal information for verification.
- What security you want to buy or sell.
- How much of the security you want to buy or sell.

Mutual fund orders are placed in terms of dollars invested. Tell the order taker, “I want to invest $5,000 in the Acme All-purpose Growth Fund, and I want to reinvest the dividends and capital gains.” That means whenever the fund pays a dividend, you will receive additional shares of the fund instead of receiving the dividend in cash. If there is a fee for purchasing the fund, you will be asked, “Do you want the fee added to the purchase price or taken out of the investment amount?” I suggest that you add the fee to the purchase so that you maximize the invested amount. In a retirement account, the fee, if any, must be paid from funds already in the account.

Orders for exchange-traded funds (ETFs) are placed for a specific number of shares. Remember, ETFs are bought and sold like a share of stock. Tell the order taker, “I want to buy X number of shares of Acme Growth ETF.” You should know the symbol of the ETF and the order taker should repeat it to you along with the full name of the ETF.

That’s it. Your order has been completed. Some firms have a separate order desk and toll-free number for investments which trade on an exchange, like stocks and ETFs, and another desk and number for mutual fund orders. When you are opening the account, ask how this is set up and get the separate toll-free numbers.

Don't get locked up trying to select an investment firm. Although investment firms are generally viewed as falling into one of three categories (brokerage, mutual fund company, or banking), they all can offer the same products and services. Check their reputation.

Dollar Cost Averaging

Dollar cost averaging is the term for investing the same amount of money into an investment at regular intervals. For example, purchasing $100 of the XYZ Growth Fund each month.

Dollar cost averaging disciplines our investing by creating a steady investment pattern, regardless of what the stock or bond markets are doing. When the share price is down, you will purchase more shares of the fund. As the price goes up, the same dollar investment will purchase fewer shares. This helps prevent buying high and selling low. It also eliminates our chances of letting our emotions guide our investing habits. Remember Rule 1, Know Yourself. Nobody likes to buy during down markets when the outlook is the darkest, but those periods offer great investing opportunities for long-term investors. Dollar cost averaging is the slow and steady route to building a solid long-term portfolio and fits well with my Hound Dog Portfolio described in Chapter 10.

Ask your investment firm about setting up dollar cost averaging for the funds you have chosen. All of the mutual fund companies offer this service as do most of the brokerage firms. Set a specific dollar amount for automatic monthly investment. The firm will debit your checking or savings account for the monthly amount at no additional cost to you. There is usually a minimum dollar amount required for this automatic investment. Typically, IRAs will require at least $25 or $50 per month; a taxable account usually requires more. This information is available at the mutual fund's web site and in the fund's prospectus. When setting up an automatic investment plan in an IRA, be sure you do not exceed your annual contribution limits.

Where to Stash the Cash

A last consideration in the implementation process is what to do with the cash. Where do you put your savings and investable money?

Cash may be good to have around and comforting knowing that it's in the bank, but cash is not an investment. You may be asking, "If our goal is to have money to spend in our retirement, then why is cash so bad?" The simple reality is the purchasing power of our money declines every year. In August 2008, the Bureau of Labor Statistics reported that the Consumer Price Index (CPI) rose 5.7% in the twelve months since July 2007! By the end of 2008, the CPI dropped below zero for a few months. But over time the CPI has hovered at or above 3% annually.

Check out the current CPI at the Bureau of Labor Statistics' home page: www.bls.gov/CPI/.

The impact of the CPI and inflation on our cash results in the decline in the purchasing power of our money. I am sure this is not news to anyone. Recall your first car. What did it cost? How about a gallon of gas for that car?

Places for your cash:

- Checking account - always available (liquid), but a poor choice for keeping any significant balance. The lowest rate of interest paid. Normally does not keep up with the impact of inflation.
- Money Market account - always available (liquid); for savings and some of our emergency cash reserves. Low interest rate which usually will not match the inflation rate.
- Certificates of Deposit (CD) - not liquid; rate is fixed for the term of the CD; better interest rate than money market accounts. Good place for our emergency cash reserves using short-term CDs.

Everyone needs to set aside an emergency cash reserve equal to three to six months for living expenses, for those unanticipated events in life. But after the emergency reserve is funded, the remainder of our investable income needs to be directed into *investing for retirement*. Review Section 2 for details on taking a financial snapshot to see where you are financially and how much you have left over for saving and investing.

While you are accumulating funds for investment purchases and IRA contributions, I recommend that you keep your investable reserves in a money market account, presumably earning a higher rate of interest than your checking account. However, every few months check the yield on your money market account. It's not unusual for the rates on these accounts to fluctuate widely and frequently and become uncompetitive. It's your money; keep it working as hard for you as you did to earn it.

Chapter Questions

1. What are the securities laws of the United States designed to protect?

2. Find at least two Internet sites which provide the investor with official regulatory information about brokers and dealers (firms).

3. List types of investment firms which offer a full line of investing choices.

4. List the three general groups of investment accounts, as defined in this chapter.

5. List two different types of IRA accounts. What are their primary differences?

6. Which retirement accounts offer tax-free withdrawals? Which accounts are tax-deferred?

7. What investment choices are offered to investors at brokerage companies?

8. What investment choices are offered to investors at mutual fund companies? At Banks and credit unions?

9. What is dollar cost averaging?

10. What are the advantages of using dollar cost averaging?

11. Why is holding cash not a good investment?

12. Where can you go to learn the Consumer Price Index for the last 12 months? What is the CPI for the last 12 months?

13. What affect did the CPI have on your cash, checking, and money market accounts? On your CD and investment accounts?

14. What can you do with your investment cash while you accumulate funds for investing?

Chapter 12
Individual Retirement Accounts (IRAs)

Chapter Objectives

- Understand the difference between tax-deferred and tax-free.
- Know IRA contribution limits and restrictions.
- Understand how to avoid IRA withdrawal penalties.
- See the advantage of an IRA conversion.
- Understand inherited IRA choices.

Definition and Details

The Individual Retirement Account (IRA) was created by the Employee Retirement Income Security Act (ERISA) in 1974. Originally, IRAs were limited to an annual contribution of $1,500 for employees not covered by a qualified employer sponsored retirement plan.

Over the last 30 plus years, Congress has expanded and modified IRAs through a series of legislation. The Economic Recovery Tax Act of 1981 increased the maximum contribution to $2,000 and added a $250 account for a non-working spouse. It also expanded the eligibility to include all taxpayers under 70½ regardless of employer retirement plan coverage. Later legislation included the Tax Reform Act of 1986, the Taxpayer Relief Act of 1997, and the Economic Growth and Tax Relief Reconciliation Act of 2001, among others.

From their beginning in 1974, IRAs have grown in scope and importance. The IRS now calls them Individual Retirement Arrangements (IRA). Today, the IRA is a key component for anyone who desires a lifestyle in retirement above the subsistence level that Social Security will provide. Regardless of the availability or scope of an employer's retirement plan, everyone can save and participate in their own retirement planning with an IRA.

Managing your IRA well and integrating it into your total investment planning is essential to achieving your goals for retirement.

Your IRA and any employer-sponsored defined-contribution retirement plan, such as a 401(k), for which you make the investment decisions, should be seen as components of your total portfolio. Include the investments in both your IRA and employer-defined contribution retirement plan when determining how much you have in each asset class.

It's not necessary to have each plan equally allocated with your desired asset allocation. You may find it easier to keep either the IRA or the retirement plan invested in fixed-income assets, while the other is primarily invested in equities. The asset allocation in each plan should be determined by the investment choices offered in the employer's plan and the options offered for distributions once you retire. With self-directed IRAs held at a brokerage firm, mutual fund company, or bank's brokerage unit, you can easily select investments which will balance the asset allocation you want for your total portfolio.

Starting in 2008, the maximum contribution level for IRAs was \$5,000 or 100% of your earned income (wages), whichever is smaller. Individuals and non-working spouses who are 50 or older may also make a $1,000 "Maximum Catch-Up Contribution." Contribution levels have been indexed to inflation since 2008.

The income and capital gains generated in an IRA are not taxed when they are earned. However, the withdrawals may be taxable. There are two major tax classifications for IRAs:

- **Tax-deferred** - taxes are due when monies are withdrawn.
  Traditional IRA - contributions may or may not be tax deductible.
  SEP IRA - employer makes contributions to individual's account.
  Simple IRA - employer and employee make contributions - similar to a 401(k).
- **Tax-free** - there are no taxes imposed on any qualified withdrawal.
  Roth IRA - contributions are not tax deductible; withdrawals are tax-free when the contribution has been in the account for 5 years or more and you are 59½ or older.

The greatest advantage of IRAs is their special tax treatment. The gains and earnings of the IRA are left in the account to grow undisturbed by taxes. Because of the tax-deferral or tax-free nature of IRAs, avoid investing your IRA in tax-favored investments, such as tax-free bonds or annuities. Your IRA is already getting the favorable tax treatment. Why place a lower yielding tax-free investment or a high-expense annuity in an already tax-favored account? There is no reason to do so.

Who may set up an IRA and at what level may they contribute?

- Traditional IRA - anyone up to the maximum contribution level, who is not yet 70½ by year end and has the following compensation.

  Wages, salaries, professional fees, bonuses, tips, commissions.

  Self-employment income.

  Taxable-alimony and separate maintenance.

  Nontaxable combat pay.

- Roth IRA - anyone who is not yet 70½ by year end, has taxable compensation and if:

  Single or head of household tax filer status - Adjusted Gross Income is…

    less than $107,000: the maximum contribution;

    between $107,000 and $122,000: a partial contribution;

    $122,000 or more: you cannot contribute to a Roth IRA.

  Joint filers or qualifying widower tax filer status - Adjusted Gross Income is…

    less than $169,000: the maximum contribution;

    between $169,000 and $179,000: a partial contribution;

    $179,000 or more: you cannot contribute to a Roth IRA.

How much may you contribute annually to an IRA?

You must have taxable compensation (earned income) during the current tax year in order to contribute to an IRA. The contribution may be up to 100% of earned income or the maximum contribution limit, whichever is smaller. The contribution may be split between a traditional and a Roth IRA, as allowed by the contribution restrictions.

Currently, the maximum contribution limit is:

- If you are under 50 years of age, the limit is $5,000.
- If you are 50 years of age or older, the limit is $6,000.

Deductibility of contributions to an IRA

- Traditional IRA - based on your income and participation in an employer retirement plan, your contribution may be deductable for the tax year you make the contribution.
- Roth IRA: contributions are not deductible.

For updated IRS limits on income eligibility and contribution deductibility, see IRS Publication 590. The publication is online at www.irs.gov/publications/p590.

All assets in an IRA must be held by a custodial firm that conforms to IRS regulations. Types of financial organizations which may act as custodian for an IRA are…

- Brokerage firms, mutual fund companies.
- Federally insured banks, savings associations, and credit unions.

- Life insurance companies.
- An entity approved by the IRS to act as trustee or custodian.

Although IRS regulations permit you to own an annuity in the IRA, you should avoid using an annuity. IRAs are tax-deferred accounts and do not need an annuity to achieve the tax-deferral. Additionally, annuities are high expense products which over time will reduce the return in accounts such as IRAs. See Chapter 20 for details concerning the proper role of annuities in your retirement planning.

The IRS imposes additional restrictions on IRAs. You cannot…

- Borrow money from your IRA.
- Sell property to your IRA.
- Buy property for personal use with your IRA funds.
- Use it as security for a loan.

The IRS will impose penalties and additional taxes on your IRA if you…

- Take early distributions.
- Make excess contributions.
- Invest in collectibles.
- Overstate the amount of nondeductible contributions.
- Fail to file Form 8606, if required.

Earnings and rollovers to a Roth IRA must remain in the account five years before you take them out, or you may be charged a 10% early distribution penalty. Distributions from a Roth IRA are penalty free if they were taken after the five-year waiting period, and any one of the following:

- Made on or after you reach 59½.
- You are disabled.
- For the purchase of a first home (up to $10,000).
- Made to a beneficiary or your estate after your death.
- For other IRS approved financial hardships.

With all the advantages that a traditional IRA offers, should you consider a Roth IRA in your investment planning? Absolutely. Who doesn't want tax-free earnings on their investments? Or tax-free withdrawals from their retirement plans? The Roth IRA provides both: tax-free growth and earnings, and tax-free withdrawals. The Roth IRA, unlike the traditional IRA, does not require you to begin to withdraw monies from the account once you reach 70½. If you don't need the money, leave it in the account for later withdrawal or pass it on to your beneficiaries.

Everyone who is eligible to contribute to a Roth IRA should have one. This is especially true for younger investors who have more time to let their investments grow tax-free. For investors of any age, the compounding affect and freedom to decide when, if ever, to take withdrawals, offers a great advantage over the traditional IRA.

Required Minimum Distributions

The IRS requires you to take minimum distributions from your deferred retirement accounts after you reach 70½. These distributions are called Required Minimum Distributions, or RMDs. Your deferred retirement accounts are your IRAs and employer sponsored defined-contribution retirement plans. Deferred refers to the fact that taxes were not paid on the income you contributed to those accounts, and/or the earnings on the accounts were not taxed during the year they were earned. In other words, the taxes were deferred, and once you reach 70½, it's time to settle up with the taxman.

Rules for Required Minimum Distributions:

- Must begin by April 1 of the year following the year you turn 70½.
- Amount of the distribution is calculated using your:
  Age and life expectancy, and
  IRA balance (all IRAs) as of December 31 of preceding year.
- Penalty of 50% on the RMD if you fail to take the distribution, not take enough, or take it late.
- RMD waived if you are 70½ and still working for an employer.

The custodian of your IRA and defined contribution plan should calculate the RMD amount for you each year. Calculate your RMD to help with planning and see where other sources of income might best come from. Check the IRS Publication 590, www.irs.gov/publications/p590, for additional information, rules, and worksheets regarding RMDs.

Converting Traditional IRA to Roth IRA

IRA investors must also decide whether or not to convert their traditional IRA to a Roth IRA and take advantage of tax-free growth and withdrawals. The tax code, with certain restrictions, allows you to convert all or a portion of your traditional IRA into a Roth IRA. If you convert, you must pay the taxes on the appreciated value greater than your cost basis. Your cost basis is the total of your contributions which you did not deduct from your taxes over the years. For example, if you contributed $35,000 to your IRA, and you were able to deduct $20,000 of those contributions from your income, then your cost basis is $15,000. You have already paid taxes on the $15,000, which you did not deduct; so you won't be taxed again on that money.

The Tax Increase Prevention and Reconciliation Act of 2005 (TIPRA) removed any income limitation on who may convert an IRA, beginning in 2010. In addition, TIPRA allowed you to spread the reportable income from a conversion made in 2010 over 2 years (2011 and 2012 tax years) if you chose.

The Crash of 2008 and 2009 took a toll on many IRAs. If the current value of your accounts is still significantly diminished, with the cost basis static, the potential tax on the conversation is greatly reduced. Converting some portion or all of your traditional IRA, will allow your IRA to recover in a tax-free account, your future withdrawals to be tax-free, and let you decide when to take withdrawals after you reach 70½.

If you decide to convert your IRA, keep in mind that "you must roll over into the Roth IRA the same property you received from the traditional IRA."[19] This means that if you withdraw money, securities, or other IRA investments, you must roll them back into the Roth IRA. If you take possession of the assets, you must roll them over within 60 days or you will pay the tax or early withdrawal penalty. To avoid this possibility let your custodian transfer the assets into the Roth IRA for you. Remember, you don't have to sell securities and transfer cash when converting your IRA. You may instruct the custodian to move securities from your traditional IRA into your Roth IRA. This will eliminate the brokerage cost to sell and repurchase the securities.

When deciding whether or not to convert your IRA, keep in mind the tax implications. Will it push you into a higher tax bracket? If you are retiring, will it increase your adjusted income to a level that will increase your Medicare premium? Currently, there is a Medicare Part B premium increase for incomes above $170,000.

Conversions to a Roth IRA must be held in the account for 5 years, or until you turn 59½, whichever comes first, or the withdrawals are subject to the 10% withdrawal penalty. Earnings must be held in the account for 5 years to be penalty free. Once you turn 59½, and the Roth IRA has been opened for 5 years, you can make withdrawals penalty free without regard to contributions or earnings since all withdrawals are considered to come first from contributions.

IRAs play an important role in your retirement planning. Their importance cannot be overstated. They provide the means to save and invest for the future in a tax-deferred or tax-free account. Once you have contributed to your employer's retirement plan, your IRA should be the next retirement savings and investment contribution that you make.

If you are qualified to contribute to a Roth IRA and can afford to bypass the traditional IRA contribution tax deduction, take advantage of a tax-free future with a Roth IRA. The Roth won't get you a tax deduction, but it will pay off many times over when you take those tax-free withdrawals.

Passing on Your IRA

IRAs are not only a great investment and retirement account for you, but also for your heirs. Anyone fortunate enough to not need all the assets of their IRA for expenses during retirement may leave the balance to one or more beneficiaries. The beneficiary may be anyone—your spouse, children, friend, anyone.

You should specify a primary beneficiary(s) for your IRA, and optionally a secondary beneficiary(s). Secondary beneficiaries inherit the account only if they outlive you and your primary beneficiary. You may specify more than one person as the primary and secondary beneficiaries and indicate what percentage of the account you want to go to each beneficiary.

Your beneficiaries will have several options for the inherited IRA. They may choose to…

- Receive a lump sum distribution, or
- Transfer the assets to an IRA and begin receiving distributions based upon their life expectancy.

Spouses have an additional option: they may choose to be treated as the owner instead of a beneficiary. This will allow them to either assume ownership of the inherited IRA, or roll it over into their own IRA and take distributions, if required, based upon their age. This is especially advantageous for younger spouses who do not currently need additional income.

If you do not designate a person as a beneficiary, and the IRA goes to your estate, the balance of the IRA must be distributed within five years to the heirs of your estate, and the option to take distributions over someone's life expectancy is lost.

If your Roth IRA is passed on to anyone other than your spouse, the assets in the IRA are included in your taxable estate and may be subject to estate taxes if your estate exceeds the estate tax exemption in effect at the date of your death.

Depending upon who is the beneficiary, the treatment and choice of distributions for a Roth IRA are different:

- Spouse beneficiary -
    - May elect to take ownership of the Roth IRA, or
    - May elect to receive distributions as any beneficiary (see below).

- Non-spouse beneficiary -
    - All distributions must be received by the fifth year following your death, or received over the beneficiary's life. Usually the choice is made by the beneficiary if not made prior by you when the IRA was established.
    - Additional contributions by the beneficiary to the IRA are not permitted.

- Distributions of earnings are subject to taxes and penalty if taken before the fifth year after the original IRA was established. After the fifth year, all distributions are tax-free.

If you are uncertain of the tax impact of an Individual Retirement Account and its options, consult with a tax specialist, accountant, or the Internal Revenue Service for assistance in determining the specific affect on your tax situation.

Chapter Questions

1. What is the difference between a tax-deferred and a tax-free account?

2. Who may set up and contribute to a traditional IRA?

3. What are the Roth IRA eligibility restrictions?

4. Are all traditional IRA contributions tax deductible? Are Roth contributions deductable?

5. List some of the restricted activities on IRAs.

6. What does the five-year waiting period mean for a Roth IRA?

7. For a non-spouse beneficiary of a Roth IRA, what are the two distribution choices?

Chapter 13
Employer Retirement Plans

Chapter Objectives

- Understand the two types of employer retirement plans.
- Know the characteristics of a defined-benefit plan.
- Know the characteristics of a defined-contribution plan.
- Understand restrictions on defined-contribution plans.
- Understand your options for transferring retirement plan assets.
- Understand the importance of keeping plan communications.

Employer-sponsored retirement plans have been around since the early 1900's when the Pennsylvania Railroad offered a pension to its retirees. During most of the 20th century retirement plans, where available, were funded by the employer. In the last few decades, the funding of retirement plans has changed to emphasize an expanded role for employee contributions.

To understand the role of employer-sponsored retirement plans and how they fit into your retirement planning, let's look at the fundamentals of these plans. Employer-sponsored retirement plans are defined as one of the following:

- Defined-benefit plans - the benefit payment at retirement is a specific amount based upon an employer determined formula, such as a percentage of your average salary for each year of employment, or a specific benefit amount.

The defined-benefit plan is funded by your employer.

- Defined-contribution plans - contributions from both the employee and employer are made to an individual's separate retirement account. The benefit payment is based on the value of the account at retirement. This type of plan includes: 401(k), 403(b) and SEP plans.

Historically, defined-benefit plans were the most common. However, in the 1970's companies began to phase out defined-benefit plans replacing them with defined-contribution plans. In the last few decades, many defined-benefit plans have become financially burdensome for employers and industries as benefits, retiree longevity, and expenses increased faster than profits and employer contributions to the plans. Today, most workers are not covered by a defined-benefit plan.

To help you understand the differences, here is a brief description of these plans.

Defined-Benefit Plan

The characteristics of a defined-benefit plan are…

- Benefits are based on an employer-determined formula such as length of employment and earnings.
- Employer funds and is responsible for contributions that will provide promised benefits.
- Investments are managed by the plan officials or hired investment company.

- Participation may require a minimum age or length of employment.
- The benefit for vested employees who leave before retirement age stays with the plan until the employee reaches retirement age.
- A basic level of benefits is guaranteed by the Federal government through the Pension Benefit Guaranty Corporation.
- Benefit accruals may be reduced during future employment, but past accruals may not be taken away.

The good news about defined-benefit plans is…

- You are not responsible for managing the assets to achieve the promised benefit.
- You do not contribute to the plan.
- Some level of basic benefits is guaranteed by Pension Benefit Guaranty Corporation.

The bad news is there are not many defined-benefit plans around today.

Do not include defined-benefit plans in your investment portfolio, since you have no role in the management of those assets.

Defined-Contribution Plan

Today, most retirement plan participants are covered by a defined-contribution plan, such as…

- 401(k), Roth 401(k) - most common offered by companies.
- 403(b) - educational and nonprofit organizations.
- 457 - state and local government.
- TSP - Thrift Savings Plan for federal employees and the military.

These plans offer employees the opportunity to save and invest for retirement with automatic contributions each payday. Usually, the employer will make a minimal contribution and match a portion of the employee's contribution. If your employer offers a defined-contribution plan, it's important that you participate and that your contribution be at least the minimum amount required to receive the employer's full contribution—don't leave any money on the table.

Usually the plan participant (employee) will select the investments for the plan. Most plans include a choice of funds which offer different asset classes and investing styles. This variety of choices will help you match the investments to your risk tolerance and asset allocation.

If you are a participant in one of these plans, be sure to include these investment assets as part of your investment portfolio when managing your asset allocation.

The characteristics of a defined-contribution plan are…

- Benefits at retirement are based on the value of the investments in the individual's retirement account.
- Both employee and employer contribute.
- Employee contributions and earnings are tax-deferred until withdrawn.
- IRS and/or employer impose annual contribution limits.
- Usually the employee is responsible for the selection of investments; however with some plans the plan administrator may be responsible for the selections.
- Assets may be rolled into a self-directed IRA, transferred to another plan, left with the plan for monthly distributions, or paid out in a lump sum (not recommended).
- No federal guarantee of the assets' market value.
- Employee contributions are usually necessary in order to receive the full amount of the employer contribution.
- May impose minimum years of employment for full vesting of employer contributions.
- Employee contributions and earnings are always 100% vested.
- Some plans permit participants to borrow from the plan or take hardship distributions before retirement.

There are restrictions on defined-contribution plans. Consult your plan documents for specifics. The most universal restrictions are…

- Annual contributions limits imposed by the plan and/or the IRS.

- IRS imposes a 10% penalty for distributions before 59 ½. Exceptions: if you are at least 55 *and* terminate employment, or demonstrate "immediate and heavy financial need" that is approved by IRS.
- Must take required minimum distributions when you reach 70 ½.

Pension Protection Act of 2006

The Pension Protection Act of 2006 (PPA) makes it easier for plan sponsors to automatically enroll employees and set a default contribution rate. One of the goals for PPA is to increase participation in these defined-contribution retirement plans. This goal is slowly being met with participation growing to just under 80% at the end of 2008.

PPA permits these plans to designate default investments which are age-appropriate for the participant, such as target-date funds. Additionally plans can automatically increase the employee's contribution over time. Of course employees have the right to opt out of the plan or choose the investment selections and contribution rate. These new provisions offered through PPA will help employees who are investment-challenged or lethargic in their attempts to participate in a retirement savings plan.

Employees who have been automatically enrolled in a retirement plan need to understand how their plan assets are invested. You need to be aware of the default investment for your plan. Some plans will default to stable-value funds, money market-like funds with little or no principal fluctuation but offering little upside potential.

Other plans may default to target-date funds. If your plan uses target-date funds, be sure to check the specific allocation mix of equities and fixed income. During the stock market crash of 2008, many target-date funds were over committed to equities even as the target-date was approaching the predefined retirement date.

Ask your plan administrator or HR department for details about the choice of funds available and the default selection. Be sure your retirement assets are invested to match your desired asset allocation—it's your money and your retirement.

Transferring Retirement Plans

When you leave your job for another employer or retire, you must decide what to do with your employer-sponsored defined-contribution plan. Each plan may offer different options for leaving the assets with the plan or taking a benefit payout. Review the plan documents or ask the plan administrator for details about your options.

Before deciding what to do with your retirement plan assets, be sure you understand these issues:

- May you leave the assets in the plan?
- If retired, what are the payout options—fixed payments or as requested?
- How do the investment's annual returns compare to their benchmark indices?
- What are the expenses of the plan's current investment selections?
- Does the plan offer the investment selections which fit your

asset allocation?

You own the vested assets of the retirement plan and you may…

- Roll over the assets into the new employer's plan, if permitted by the new plan.
- Transfer the assets into a self-directed IRA, as a rollover distribution.
- Take a lump-sum distribution. You will pay taxes on the full asset distribution. This is not a recommended choice unless the asset value is minimal.

See Chapter 14, Maintaining Your Investment Plan, for additional details concerning the transfer of plan assets, what factors to consider, potential limitations, and questions to ask.

Keeping Retirement Plan Documents

Record keeping is always a hassle, but with retirement plans it's important to keep and review all communications (statements and other mailings).

In this era of mergers, acquisitions, and bankruptcies, communication between employees, retirees, and retirement plan administrators can break down. If a new plan administrator is appointed and records are not properly transferred or made available, you could experience problems with the servicing of your plan. To minimize the potential for problems, you should…

- Keep the plan administrator informed of any change in your contact information.
- Save the annual statements from your retirement plan.
- Keep copies of all communications with plan administrators.
- Be sure you are continuing to receive periodic statements.
- If the plan changes administrators or computer systems, double-check statements to be sure all assets are accounted for.

Occasionally when a company or retirement plan closes, you may not hear from your retirement plan administrator or receive benefits or communications in a timely manner. Should that happen, those saved documents will come in handy. Call or write the plan administrator at the most recent address. If after making reasonable attempts to contact the new administrator, you are unable to reach anyone, the Department of Labor may be able to help. You will need to provide documentation to back up your claim. Call the Department toll free at (866)444-3272 or go to their web site: www.dol.gov/ebsa .

Chapter Questions

1. What are the two types of employer-sponsored retirement plans?

2. List characteristics of a defined-benefit plan.

3. List characteristics of a defined-contribution plan.

4. List restrictions of a defined-contribution plan.

5. What steps should you take to help minimize problems when a retirement plan changes administrators?

Chapter 14
Maintaining Your Investment Plan

Chapter Objectives

- Understand that goals and plans may change.
- See your plans in light of the present.
- Know how to modify retirement investment goals.
- Understand the importance of rebalancing your portfolio.
- Learn how to rebalance your investment portfolio.

Periodic Reviews

One of the routines that make life interesting is that things change. Our goals can change as we move through life. Any number of events may cause the best, most carefully designed plans to need some refinement, if not major modifications. Unforeseen events will happen, and we need to be willing to make changes to our goals and plans when necessary. We need the flexibility to make changes to our retirement goals and investment plan as we move toward retirement.

I doubt anyone could have lived through the Financial Tsunami of 2008 and 2009 without knowing that the world and their financial plans had been abruptly changed. In October 2007, at the peak of the DJIA, portfolios with heavy doses of equities were generating broad gains and comforting assurances that equities would continue producing these high returns. Many investors were lulled into believing this performance would continue uninterrupted. They questioned why anyone would want to leave any money on the table by reducing their exposure to stocks. The returns may not have reached the level of the dot-com boom, but they certainly beat returns generated by increasing their fixed income allocation. Most investors were content to leave well enough alone and enjoy the ride believing they would adjust their portfolio allocation later as it became clear the bull market was coming to an end.

As I said earlier, there's an old Wall Street adage, "No one rings a bell at the top or the bottom of a market." That's why we need an asset allocation that fits our risk tolerance and that we will stick with in both up and down markets.

I recommend that you designate a specific time each year to review your goals, investment plan, and portfolio allocation. The date you choose should be one you can easily remember, such as a birth date or month. The weeks between late November and the end of the year are too hectic for most of us to be able to kick back, analyze goals, and review investment portfolios. The annual review needs to be at a time when you have minimum distractions.

During your review, evaluate how you are doing in meeting your goals. Understand and answer these questions:

- Are you saving and investing the dollars you committed to in your plan?
- Are you systematically investing?
- Have you withdrawn funds from a retirement account to meet unanticipated expenses? Have those funds been replaced?

- Are there any investments in your portfolio which are lagging their benchmark indices? If so, should they be replaced?
- Have you strayed from you established asset allocation? Do you need to rebalance your portfolio?
- Are you overexposed to an asset class? Is it time to capture some of those gains and invest them in a lagging asset class?

Many factors can cause our portfolios to get skewed and over time drift from our desired asset allocation. It's important to recognize the necessity to review our goals and investments in light of the present reality and make appropriate adjustments as required. If our goals and investment plan were realistic in the first place, the adjustments should be minimal or even unnecessary.

Answer the following questions as you review your retirement goals:

- Has my retirement date changed?
  Putting off retirement is a great way to build additional financial resources for your retirement years. If you find your financial goals are not being met, delaying retirement, if possible, is the best way to add to retirement savings. If the retirement date has moved closer, consider taking another job before retirement or part-time employment during your initial retirement years.

- Am I saving and investing enough to achieve my financial goal with respect to my retirement date?

Review your savings and investing plan. Are there additional areas for savings which could be directed into retirement plans and savings? Prepare an annual budget and cash flow analysis to help you see where your money is going and items where you could make spending adjustments.

- Is my savings and investment portfolio on track to achieve the financial goal that I set for the start of my retirement? If not, does my asset allocation need to be reviewed or adjusted?

Do an annual review of your investments and savings. See the section below for guidance with rebalancing. Assuming you will continue to save and invest as before, will the dollars be there at the start of your retirement? Is the goal you set, reasonable? Is your asset allocation reasonable in light of your financial goal? Adjustments are OK. The sooner you discover that mid-course corrections are needed, the better.

Warning: if you are not achieving your goal, don't take on more risk in order to catch up. But at the same time, don't assume zero risk. This question may require you to review Chapter 7 and set a more realistic asset allocation. Be careful. Do not get out of your risk tolerance comfort zone. Doing so may lead to loss of confidence with your plan and abandonment to your emotions during stock market peaks and dips.

- Will I be carrying any debt into retirement? If so, is it possible that I could eliminate the debt prior to retirement? Debt is not the friend of retirees. You are paying someone else for the privilege of past consumption. Eliminating debt prior to retirement is the best way to increase spendable income during your retirement years.

- Is my present job secure enough to get me to my retirement date? If not, can I increase my savings rate? Do I have a level of job skills which would help or hinder finding another job?

  Job security and longevity for employees is not what it was in past generations. If there is a reasonable chance that you may not make your retirement date in your current job, you should take steps to reduce your spending and maximize savings. Review and adjust your current spending budget, be sure you have six months of expenses set aside in available savings and take a personal inventory of your job skills and potential training opportunities.

- Could I be saving and investing more?
  This is implied in all the previous questions. If you can find the additional savings, this is the best way to prepare for retirement or a forced early retirement.

Rebalancing Your Portfolio

Periodically, it's necessary to make adjustments to our portfolio in order to maintain our desired asset allocation. As the stock market and interest rates move through the inevitable cycles, the value of the equity and bond portions of our investments will fluctuate. This fluctuation may lead to an undesirable asset allocation in a portfolio.

Rebalancing your portfolio will bring the value of the investments back into line with your selected asset allocation. As one asset class increases in value it may represent a larger percentage of your portfolio than your asset allocation calls for. Rebalancing your portfolio will force you to buy low and sell high.

Why is this necessary? To understand rebalancing, let's recall the necessity for determining a proper asset allocation in the first place. We all have an investment risk tolerance and temperament: conservative, moderate, or aggressive. As we move closer to our retirement date, we need to invest more conservatively in order to help preserve our assets and still provide for growth as we stay within our risk tolerance comfort zone. Since the stock market will always fluctuate, we will never experience a time when our emotions are neutral; they will swing between fear and greed. At times, we can become nervous about our ability to select investments and second-guess our decisions, especially during down markets when fear kicks in. The asset allocation forces us into a mix of investments which is appropriate for our risk tolerance and goals regardless of the state of the market.

Although rebalancing will help us stay with the allocation that offers the best opportunity to achieve our investment goals, it does have a potential drawback. During prolonged periods of stock market decline, rebalancing can negatively impact our portfolio if we rebalance too frequently. That is, if we sell winners and buy a losing asset class every month or two. This would force us into more losers on the way down. Therefore, an annual rebalancing is recommended (not more frequently).

Rebalancing is a straightforward process. It involves…

1. Determining your asset allocation based on the current portfolio values.
2. Comparing the current portfolio allocation to your desired asset allocation.
3. Making appropriate changes to your investments to bring your portfolio back into line with the desired allocation. That means, sell a portion of the funds in the asset class which is greater than the allocation goal, and buy more of the funds which are an asset class below the desired allocation goal; i.e., buy low and sell high.

For example, in Chapter 7, you learned that if you are 10 years away from retirement and you have a moderate risk tolerance, the asset allocation you should select is…

Large Cap	25%
Small/Mid Cap	20%
Foreign	25%
Fixed Income	30%

Assume you have a *current* total investment portfolio of $100,000, with market values for each asset class as follows:

Large Cap	$31,000	31%
Small/Mid Cap	15,000	15%
Foreign	32,000	32%
Fixed Income	22,000	22%

It's obvious that you need to rebalance your investments to get them back to the asset allocation you selected as a goal. Therefore, make adjustments to your investments as follows:

1. Sell $6000 of the Large Cap investments.
2. Sell $7,000 of the Foreign investments.
3. Purchase $5,000 additional shares of the Small/Mid Cap investments.
4. Purchase $8,000 additional shares of the Fixed Income investments.

Those adjustments will bring your asset allocation for your total investment portfolio back into line with your desired allocation. This will also help you take some money off the table (profits) in the large cap class when you sell $6,000 of those appreciated investments.

This shouldn't be a tedious or time-consuming task. If you have invested in index funds similar to those suggested in this book, your funds will be very close to matching one of the asset classes (large cap, small/mid cap, foreign, or fixed income). Be aware that some funds might have overlap among the asset classes. Check the fund's latest annual report for the asset class percentages or use one of the web sites that provides mutual fund and ETF research. They are reasonably up-to-date with fund statistics and asset class mix.

Use Table D-5A, Worksheet for Rebalancing Your Portfolio. Calculate your portfolio allocation percentages and determine which, if any, of your investments need to be bought or sold. Table D-5B, Example and Instructions for Using Worksheet for Rebalancing Your Portfolio, will give you the step-by-step instructions for rebalancing. An example of the calculation process is also included.

Annually reviewing and rebalancing your portfolio is important. The rebalancing procedure will keep your investments on track and help reduce your emotional responses to market fluctuations as you save and invest before retirement, at retirement, and during retirement.

Including Employer Retirement Plans

If you are responsible for making the investment selections in your employer-sponsored defined-contribution plan, be sure to include those investments in your total portfolio when you manage your asset allocation.

Your retirement plan sponsor provided you with a list of the available mutual funds from which you may choose. Take the time to determine the asset class for each fund from the available choices. This may take a little research, but the effort will help you maintain your portfolio's desired asset allocation. If you don't know the asset class of a retirement fund, you will not know the true state of your portfolio's asset allocation.

- Ask your employer or retirement plan sponsor for the list of investment choices.
- Ask your plan sponsor for the latest fund(s) prospectus.

- Ask your plan sponsor for a Summary Plan Description document.
- Check the fund company's web site for the latest prospectus and asset classes for the fund or ask that they send you a prospectus.
- Review annually the performance and asset classes of the funds in your plan.
- Know the expense ratio of the funds in your plan and of the available alternatives.
- Use low expense index funds for the asset classes when possible.

> Note: Investing more than 10% of your retirement plan in the stock of your employer will leave you overexposed to the health of your employer. If your employer goes out of business or files for bankruptcy, you could not only lose your job, but your investment in the company's stock as well. Your retirement portfolio needs good diversification which is not available when a major portion of your retirement assets are invested in the stock of one company. Remember Enron, the U.S. automobile companies, and several large banks for the most recent examples of employees losing their jobs and their investments in the stock of those companies.

Transferring a Retirement Plan

When you leave one job for another employer, you have the option to move your defined-contribution retirement plan to the new employer's plan or into a self-directed IRA. This is called a rollover distribution.

Your rollover distribution options are…

- Rollover distribution to the new employer plan, if the new plan will accept it.
- Rollover into an IRA.

So, should you take your retirement plan to the new employer? It depends. To understand which option is best, consider the following:

- Does your former employer permit you to leave the assets with them?
- What investment choices do the former and new employer plans offer?
- Does the new employer offer good choices for diversification and asset class mix?
- How has the return on the investments been in the new vs. old plans?
- Which plan is the least expensive? Check expense ratios.
- How do the expenses of the new and old plans compare to index funds available in a self- directed IRA at a brokerage firm or bank?
- Do you have an outstanding loan from your plan?

You may also take a lump sum distribution from the retirement plan. This is not a good choice, since taxes will be due on the full distribution instead of on smaller amounts spread out over many years. A lump sum distribution may also push you into a higher tax bracket in the year of the distribution.

As you can see from the above list, the decision should be based upon the availability of good performing, low expense-ratio funds. If the new plan does not offer both of these qualities, don't move your retirement funds to the new employer's plan. The best choice may be to keep your retirement plan with your former employer or roll it over into a self-directed IRA. All of the investment selections mentioned in this book are available through a brokerage firm, mutual fund company, or brokerage unit of a bank, savings association, or credit union.

There is another factor to consider regarding the transfer of an employer plan to an IRA. When will you need to start withdrawing the money? If you leave the assets in the old employer's plan, you can begin to withdraw money without penalty at age 55. If you transfer the assets into an IRA, you must wait to withdraw money until you are 59½, or you will pay a 10% early withdrawal penalty.

Also be aware, that if you have an outstanding loan from your 401(k), your old employer can deduct the loan from the distribution, and the IRS will impose taxes on the loan amount as if it were a taxable distribution. Check with the plan administrator for details on how they will handle any outstanding loan.

I rolled over a 401(k) into a self-directed IRA with a discount broker. Using index funds, I have achieved the diversification and asset allocation I wanted with minimal expense. Using the self-directed IRA also makes it easier for me to do the annual rebalancing of my portfolio.

While on the subject of transferring retirement plans, don't forget you can transfer your IRAs to a new custodian - although there may be transfer fees. To avoid any penalties, have the new custodial firm arrange the transfer for you. If you take delivery of the IRA assets and hold them for more than 60 days, this will be treated as a distribution and taxes can be due.

Check to be sure the new custodian can hold the assets you currently have in your IRA. Some mutual funds cannot be held by all brokerage firms. The firm must have a contract with the mutual fund company. If the new custodian can't hold the fund, you must either sell the fund and transfer cash, or stay with the current custodian.

Staying on Course

Once you have determined your asset allocation, selected and purchased your investments, and begun to make annual reviews of your investment plan and portfolio, be sure you don't drift into complacency. Retirement goals and plans can and will change. Your investments and financial circumstances will fluctuate. What started out as a reasonable plan may become outdated or unrealistic. Be willing to review, plan, and make changes as you move toward and reach that moment of retirement.

Here is a list for guidance and reminders of essential steps that will help you maintain your investment plan and reach your retirement goals.

- Prepare and review your cash flow analysis at least twice a year.
- If you are spending more than you earn, prepare a budget and stick to it.
- Purchase items on a credit card only if the balance can be paid off each month.
- Be willing to make spending adjustments as needed to maintain your desired savings rate.
- Increase your savings rate whenever possible.
- Annually rebalance your portfolio to match your desired asset allocation.
- Be sure you are contributing at least enough to receive your employer's matching retirement plan contribution.
- Set a specific time goal to get out of debt and pay off credit card balances. If at all possible, be debt-free by retirement.
- Evaluate your employment situation currently and at retirement. Should you work longer in your present job or consider a part-time job in retirement?
- Don't let the emotions of the moment and pundits in the news divert you with, "This is a new era, the old is out, new ideas or strategies are the only way to go." Remember March 2000; review Rule 1 for a reminder of the last *paradigm shift*.
- Periodically review and adjust your retirement date and goals, if necessary, to fit your financial reality.

Chapter Questions

1. Why is reviewing retirement and investing goals important?

2. List some of the important questions to answer when reviewing your goals.

3. How frequently should you review your retirement and investment goals?

4. What role does your asset allocation play in your investment review? Why is it important?

5. Why is rebalancing your portfolio important?

6. What does rebalancing you portfolio involve?

7. List the three basic steps for rebalancing your investment portfolio.

8. What are the options you have regarding the transfer of assets from a former employer's retirement plan?

9. What specific steps can you take to help you reach your retirement goals?

Chapter 15
Preparing For Retirement

Chapter Objectives

- Realize that goals may change.
- Understand how to prepare a retirement budget.
- Determine where expense items go in a budget.
- Develop a personal list of pre-retirement to-do items.

As you prepare to transition into retirement, a review of your retirement goals is important. Things change: circumstances, jobs, incomes, family situations, and retirement goals. It's not productive to keep following an old route if your destination goals have changed. If your long-term goals need adjusting, the sooner you recognize the need for change, the easier it will be to make changes that will move you toward these new goals.

Prepare a Retirement Budget

Unless you are wealthy, your income during retirement will probably not match the level of income you had during your working years. The sooner you can see that reality, the easier it will be to make adjustments to your spending and saving habits.

The first step to dealing with that reality is to prepare a realistic retirement budget, one that you can live with during retirement. Use the Retirement Budget Worksheet at the end of Appendix C to help prepare your retirement budget. As a starting point, review

Chapter 3 and the Cash Flow Worksheet you prepared in Appendix C. Analyze each expense item for reasonableness and the possibility for reduction or inclusion in your retirement lifestyle.

There will be some expense items which you should be able to reduce or eliminate, such as…

- Job related expenses -
  - Commuting, transportation.
  - Clothes for work.
  - Lunches out.
- Income replacement insurance.

At the same time, retirement will bring on new activities and expenses, such as…

- Increasing medical and prescription costs.
- Leisure and hobby pursuits; e.g., supplies, equipment, or green fees.
- Travel.
- Activities with family and friends.

Take the time to analyze each of your anticipated expenses. If there is an item which you are having trouble estimating, err on the high side. It's better to be surprised that expenses came in under the budgeted amount, than to be blind-sided by unanticipated levels of spending. It's also helpful at this point to see the full reality of retirement living expenses and income than to low- ball the expenses and experience the difficulty of balancing expenses with income after retirement has started.

The Retirement Budget Worksheet in Appendix C provides space for estimating your retirement income. Include all sources of income which you anticipate during retirement:

- Social Security.
- Defined-benefit pensions: company, union, teacher retirement plans.
- Defined-contribution retirement plans: 401(k), 403(b), other vested retirement plans.
- Withdrawals from IRAs.
- Savings and investment income: interest, and dividends.
- Annuity and insurance payments.
- Part or full-time work.
- Royalties, rents.
- Any *steady* source of income.

The list of income sources will be unique to your situation. A word of caution: don't be overly optimistic when estimating income levels from sources which are not already known. For example, dividends, interest, and royalties can be quite volatile, especially over 10, 20, or more years. Remember what happened to some long-established dividends and interest yields on CDs in 2009. For retirees, the cuts were painful.

As a starting point for estimating withdrawals from IRAs, 401(k)s, and other investment accounts, assume a conservative 4% withdrawal rate. A 4% withdrawal rate gives you a high degree of probably that you will not outlive your savings and investments. You can always adjust the withdrawal rate later as you refine the income and expense items during retirement.

Your initial retirement budget needs to be realistic. Make the effort to get as close as possible to the actual income and expenses that you will experience during your first year of retirement. Income and expenses are moving targets, but if you are not even in the ballpark with your estimates, budgeting is a waste of time.

See Chapter 19 - Establishing a Withdrawal Plan, for a further explanation of the affects of inflation, compound interest, and various withdrawal rate scenarios and their impact on your portfolio.

Utilizing a Retirement Checklist

I'm sure you know by now, I'm a list person. Lists help me to stay on track, stay focused, and as I can attest, prevent forgetting crucial steps. The following checklist is a starting point in your preparation for retirement. Review these action steps along with the Investing for Retirement Checklist in Appendix A. Make adjustments to the checklist as your particular circumstances warrant.

1. As soon as you feel it's appropriate, advise your employer of your retirement date. The more lead time you and the human resources department have to deal with the various details, the better.

2. Contact the Social Security Administration, or review your latest Social Security statement, to make sure your personal information and salary history are correct. Review the information in Chapter 14 regarding Social Security.

3. If you are one of the fortunate who has an employer-sponsored defined-benefit retirement plan, ask for the payout options—lump sum or monthly annuity payments—and a written estimate of the monthly benefit (payout). Be sure you meet any vesting requirements for owning the benefits. Generally, due to tax implications, you should not take the payout as one lump sum.

4. Ask for written details of any employer-sponsored health, Medicare supplement, and life insurance plans which you may take into retirement. Get an explanation of the benefits of each plan and any costs which you will be required to pay. Do you need to continue paying for the protection which insurance affords your dependents once you retire?

5. Decide if you should begin taking a distribution from your defined-contribution employer-sponsored retirement plan or leave the money in the plan until later. Ask if this is an option. Usually you can leave the money in the plan until you reach 70½.

6a. If you plan to continue working at another employer, ask about the possibility of transferring a defined-contribution retirement plan (401(k)) into the new employer's plan. The advisability of doing this does not lend itself to a universal recommendation. The plans must be compared to determine whether it is best to transfer out or leave the money in the former employer's plan. Check the plans for the selection of funds available, expense ratios, and annual costs. It's not a good idea to leave or place your retirement funds in the stock of the old or the new employer; think Enron for the consequences of such a decision. You need more diversification than one stock will provide.

6b. You should also consider rolling your defined-contribution retirement plan (401(k) or 403(b)) into a self-directed IRA. Using index mutual funds and ETFs, you can achieve a well-balanced, diversified portfolio with minimal expenses.

If you decide to transfer or rollover your retirement funds, be sure you do not receive the cash. The funds should be transferred or rolled over directly between custodial firms. If you receive the money, you must deposit it with another custodian within 60 days, or the IRS will treat this distribution as current income, and taxes will be due.

See Chapter 13 for more information about transferring your retirement plan.

7. Review your portfolio and asset allocation. Your risk tolerance should now be that of someone who is entering retirement.

8. Prepare a retirement budget and review your withdrawal options for retirement. Be sure to take into account the Required Minimum Distribution if you are 70½.

9. Ask if your employer offers any additional benefits to retirees such as meals, events, retiree club organizations, health screenings, or newsletters.

10. Get the name, address, and phone number of a contact in the human resources department who is designated to handle retiree questions and communications.

11. Stay connected. Join your employer's retiree club if one exists. Reconnect with alumni organizations from your college or high school. Locate groups of retirees from your church, social, or hobby organizations. Social contact and interaction is an important part of a healthy retirement.

Chapter Questions

1. What is the purpose of preparing a retirement budget?

2. Is your list of sources of income in retirement complete? Is it realistic?

3. List current expense items which can be eliminated from your retirement budget.

4. List expense items which you could reduce if necessary.

5. How many months in advance of your retirement does your employer's human resources department suggest

that you submit your retirement notice and begin filling out the paperwork?

6. How many months in advance of your retirement should you contact the Social Security Administration?

7. Make a list of personal decisions you will need to make prior to retirement.

Chapter 16
Social Security and Retirement

Chapter Objectives

- See the role of Social Security in your retirement plan.
- Understand the Social Security eligibility rules.
- Understand what full retirement age means.
- See what your Social Security is worth.
- Understand the issues of earned income and Social Security benefits.
- Understand factors that affect when to start taking Social Security.

Social Security is one government program that touches all of us—rich and poor, working or retired. And unless you have just landed on the planet, you could not have missed the news and rumors about Social Security—the problems and concerns for its future.

The problems Social Security faces have been caused by decades of optimistic political decisions. But in spite of our politicians' good intentions, the reality is that promises of future benefits have been made without the means to deliver them.

I am an optimist. I believe that what politicians have broken, politicians can fix. I also believe that Congress will do nothing to fix Social Security until the pain of reality is so great that the voters finally insist that Congress fix it.

I believe that Social Security in some form will be there for future generations as part of their retirement income. But, to assure that it will be will require Congress to make significant changes to its present funding and promises. After all, Congress came up with almost a trillion dollars in 2008 and additional trillions in 2009 for the recession. So I'm optimistic that Congress will retool Social Security programs to provide future retirees with *modest retirement income.*

Let's now focus on how to incorporate Social Security into your retirement planning.

What is Social Security?

Social Security was originally a government sponsored retirement savings plan. Old Age, Survivors and Disability Insurance Program is the official name for Social Security. The Social Security website tells us - "The Social Security Act was signed by President Franklin Roosevelt on August 14, 1935. Taxes were collected for the first time in January 1937 and the first one-time, lump-sum payments were made that same month. Regular ongoing monthly benefits started in January 1940."

Today, Social Security not only pays retirement benefits, but also disability, death, survivor, and supplemental security income to adults and children with limited resources. The Social Security Administration also assists the Department of Health and Human Services to determine Medicare eligibility and receives the Medicare premiums from workers and retirees.

Social Security is a government administered retirement annuity that pays eligible recipients and their spouses a lifetime stream of income with annual cost of living adjustments (COLA). The COLA is the increase in the Bureau of Labor Statistic, CPI-W, from the third quarter of the previous year to the third quarter of the current year. The COLA takes effect with the December Social Security payment each year.

For additional information about the full programs of the Social Security Administration (SSA), go to their web site at www.socialsecurity.gov. The site also explains in detail the history of Social Security and the computation of the earnings and quarterly credit at www.socialsecurity.gov/OACT/COLA/QC.html. For Medicare information and questions go to www.medicare.gov/default.asp.

What is Required for Eligibility?

To be eligible to receive Social Security retirement benefits, you must have accumulated 40 credits, 10 years of Social Security withholding. Beginning in 1978, employers switched to reporting earnings on an annual basis. Since that time, credits earned have been based on your total wages and self-employment income. Each year the amount of earnings required is adjusted; for the year 2011, $1,120 in earnings earned one credit, $4,480 earned the annual maximum of four credits. If you pay Social Security tax on income, it will count toward this earnings amount. Your income from savings and investments is not counted toward Social Security credits. You must be at least 62 years old to receive your Social Security retirement benefits.

A spousal benefit is available once a worker begins receiving a retirement benefit. The spouse must be at least 62 years old or have a child under his or her care who is under the age of 16 or is receiving a Social Security disability benefit. The spousal benefit can be as much as half the retiree's benefit. When the spouse has his or her own Social Security benefit, the higher benefit will be paid. To determine a spousal benefit for your particular situation, go to the SSA web site and use the spousal benefit calculator at https://www.socialsecurity.gov/OACT/quickcalc/spouse.html.

There are certain types of employment that do not count toward your eligibility credits or that may reduce your Social Security benefits. For example, if you worked for federal[20], state, or local[21] governments and did not pay Social Security taxes on those earnings, the pension you receive from those agencies may reduce your Social Security benefits. If you are unsure whether Social Security was withheld on your earnings, check with the government agency which employed you.

What Is the Full Retirement Age?

The Full Retirement Age is SSA-speak for the age at which you can start receiving "full or normal" benefits. Your full retirement age is a baseline for calculating your "full" dollar benefit based upon your highest 35 years of earnings. An SSA formula is applied to your earnings to determine the amount of your full monthly benefit.

However, if you start collecting your Social Security benefit *before* your full retirement age, SSA will reduce your full benefit. You may also wait to start collecting your benefit past your full retirement age. If you wait, your monthly benefit will increase for each month that you defer until you reach age 70. For details, see "When should you start receiving Social Security?" below.

The *full retirement age* is based on your year of birth:

Year of Birth	Full Retirement Age
1937 or earlier	65
1938	65 and 2 months
1939	65 and 4 months
1940	65 and 6 months
1941	65 and 8 months
1942	65 and 10 months
1943 - 1954	66
1955	66 and 2 months
1956	66 and 4 months
1957	66 and 6 months
1958	66 and 8 months
1959	66 and 10 months
1960 and later	67

What Is My Social Security Worth?

Have you ever pondered the question, "What is my Social Security worth?" It does have value. It is, after all, your money that's being held. To understand this question, let's ask it another way: "What would it take to replace Social Security in my investment portfolio?"

Think of Social Security as the forced purchase of a fixed annuity over a lifetime of work. It's a fixed annuity which will not only provide you with monthly income for the rest of your life and the life of your surviving spouse, but will increase over time, adjusting for the rise in consumer prices (CPI-W).

It really is a good deal. Maybe you would have earned more over 40 years in an index fund, but that was not an option. It is what it is. And it is a vital component of everyone's retirement portfolio.

To put a value on your Social Security retirement benefit requires taking a look at what it would cost you to purchase a fixed annuity with similar benefits. A fixed annuity, for a 65-year-old with a 62-year-old spouse, paying $1,200 a month for as long as either of them lived (Joint Life), would cost approximately $211,000. Factor in the guaranteed cost of living increases, and the value is even greater. This is an approximate figure using 2009 data.

When Should You Start Receiving Social Security?

When should you start receiving Social Security? This question does not have a universal answer that will fit everyone. Among the many individual factors that you should consider, are…

- Your financial situation (amount of savings and investments).
- Sources and amount of other retirement income.
- What portion of your anticipated expenses your Social Security benefit will cover.
- How much income your savings and investments will generate.
- Your health.
- Enjoyment in your present job. Do you want to continue to work? Could you continue to work?
- Your family circumstances and obligations.
- Your desire or need to earn income after retirement.

If you choose to start receiving your Social Security benefit early, your full benefit will be reduced. The reduction increases on a sliding scale for each month that you begin receiving your benefit before your full retirement age. If you begin collecting your benefit at age 62, the reduction is between 20% and 30%, depending upon your date of birth[22]. See details below.

If you choose to defer receiving your Social Security benefit past your full benefit age, the benefit will increase each month, at an annual rate of 8%, until you reach 70 or start receiving your benefit. That's a good return for any fixed income investment, especially a government backed investment.

Penalty for Taking Social Security Early

If you take Social Security early, SSA will impose a penalty on your full benefit. SSA will reduce your benefit by…

- five-ninths of 1% for each month before your full retirement age up to 36 months, and
- an additional five-twelfths of 1% for each additional month greater than 36 months before your full retirement age.

  For example, a person age 62 will have the benefit reduced 25%:

  66 - 62 = 4 years or 48 months:

(5/9 of 1%) times 36 months	= 20%
(5/12 of 1%) times 12 months	= 5%
Total reduction	= 25%

  Therefore, if your full retirement age benefit is $1,500 a month, SSA would reduce it by 25%, or $375, for a monthly benefit of $1125.

Deferring Social Security

Would you receive more in Social Security benefits if you waited to start receiving Social Security? There is no way to know absolutely, but here are some factors to keep in mind:

- If you start early, the benefit is permanently reduced, but you receive money sooner.

- If you defer past your full retirement age, benefits increase 8% per year until you begin to take your benefit, or reach age 70.
- If you live past age 78, the cumulative increased benefit will overtake what you would have received if you started taking your benefit early.

SSA has calculated the benefit, at whatever age you start to receive benefits, based upon an average life expectancy. The longer you live past your life expectancy, the more you will receive in cumulative Social Security benefits; therefore a decision to wait to start receiving benefits would be better. The important factors to consider here are your retirement income needs and your health. Ultimately, this is a very personal decision that only you can make.

The Bureau of Labor Statistics reported[23] in the summer of 2008, that 16% of the population 65 and older was still working. Over the last decade there has been a slight increase in the trend to work longer. And the impact of the recent financial crisis, will no doubt push many boomers to retire later.

Social Security May Be Taxable

Your Social Security benefits may be taxable. The SSA uses a formula which adds half of your Social Security to all of your other income to determine a taxable income threshold.

Your Social Security benefit is taxable if:

Adjusted Gross Income (from tax return 1040), plus any tax-exempt interest, plus half of your Social Security benefit for:

Joint filers -

- exceeds $32,000, 50% is taxable.
- exceeds $44,000, up to 85% is taxable.

Single filers -

- exceeds $25,000, 50% is taxable.
- exceeds $34,000, up to 85% is taxable.

Use IRS Publication 915 for a worksheet to determine the specific taxable amount of your Social Security benefit.

Penalty for Continuing to Work

There is another "got-cha" in the when-to-start-social-security decision. The income you earn after you begin to receive your Social Security benefit can be an issue. You may lose some of your Social Security benefit if your earned income exceeds certain limits and you are younger than your full retirement age.

Your decision concerning employment after starting Social Security benefits will require careful planning and budgeting estimations. Refer to your retirement budget to determine if it will be necessary to continue working to supplement your income. My advice is to err on the side of continued employment before retirement and to defer Social Security. You will not be penalized for waiting to receive Social Security, up to age 70, but you could lose some benefits if you misjudge your earnings requirements and are forced to return to the workforce.

Here is the formula SSA uses to calculate the reduction of your monthly benefit.[24] You will fall into one of these three age-based scenarios:

- If you are under your full retirement age, you will lose $1 of benefits for every $2 you earn above the annual earnings limit. For 2011, the annual earnings limit is $14,160.

- In the year you reach your full retirement age, you will lose $1 for every $3 you earn above an annual limit, earned before the month you reach full retirement age. For 2011, the year-of-full-retirement annual limit is $37,680.

- Beginning with the month you reach your full retirement age, there is no reduction in benefits regardless of your earned income.

Applying for Social Security Benefits

You should apply for Social Security benefits at least three months in advance. With over 10,000 boomers a day becoming eligible for Social Security, the Social Security Administration (SSA) is understandably encouraging new retirees to apply online. The SSA offices are not equipped to handle the caseload of applicants in the traditional manner of visiting the office in person to apply.

The SSA web site (www.ssa.gov/retire2/applying8.htm) offers the following options for applying for Social Security, along with extensive Q&As on the application process:

- Online: https://secure.ssa.gov/apps6z/iRRet/rib.
- By phone: (800) 772-1213.
- TTY phone: (800) 325-0778.
- In person: with prior appointment.

Don't forget your documentation. Depending upon your individual situation or status, you will need to bring (or submit) some original or certified documentation which could include:

- Social Security card.
- Certified birth certificate.
- Proof of US citizenship, if born outside the United States.
- Military discharge papers if you had military service before 1968.
- W-2 from last year or last year's tax return.

Chapter Questions

1. List two eligibility requirements to begin receiving Social Security retirement benefits.

2. For Social Security purposes, what is your full retirement age?

3. List factors you should consider before making the decision to begin or defer receiving your Social Security benefit?

4. Using the Social Security Administrations website, and your date of birth, find the income limits for taxing benefits at 63 years old, 65 years old and 68 years old.

Chapter 17
Medicare and Retirement

Chapter Objectives

- Know when you are eligible for Medicare.
- Understand the Parts of Medicare and what they cover.
- Know what out-of-pocket expenses to expect.
- Know which coverages require premiums and co-pays.
- Determine if supplemental Medicare insurance is desirable.

Ask most people, "What is Medicare?" or "What medical services does Medicare cover?" and you will most likely get a deer-in-the-headlights stare. Ask how it affects our parents and you may get a polite smile or quick response: "Thank God my parents are able to deal with it themselves."

Are they really? Do you know what Medicare covers? Will you be able to take advantage of the medical insurance that you have already paid for? Will you be able to determine if a Medicare supplement is worth the cost?

It's not likely that most of us will be able to understand the details of Medicare without a little help. This chapter will dissect the details and provide an outline of this most important socially sensitive government program—a program that affects each one of us.

What Is Medicare?

Medicare is a government sponsored health insurance program for people age 65 and over. It also covers people younger than 65 who are disabled and receive Social Security or Railroad Retirement Board disability benefits and anyone with End-Stage Renal disease.

Medicare was signed into law in July 1965. The Department of Health and Human Services administers the Medicare and Medicaid programs. Medicaid is a joint federal and state program which funds health care for low income individuals. The Social Security Administration is charged with determining Medicare eligibility and accounting for Medicare premium payments.

A payroll tax of 2.9% on your wages is collected as a Medicare tax. The tax is imposed on all of your wages, unlike Social Security contributions which end after wages reach an annual limit. You and your employer each pay half of the tax (1.45% each).

Depending upon the level of participation that each of us chooses, the Medicare program can cover care for medical treatment (doctors), hospitalization, and prescribed drugs.

Medicare Eligibility

Anyone is eligible for Medicare who meets both of the following criteria:

- You are at least 65 years of age and a citizen or permanent resident of the United States for 5 years.
- You or your spouse worked at least 10 years in Medicare-covered employment (i.e., paid the Medicare tax).

Additionally, you may qualify if you are younger than 65 and you have a disability or End-Stage Renal Disease and receive Social Security or Railroad Board disability benefits. You may be qualified under certain other very specific conditions; see the Medicare web site for further details on eligibility (www.medicare.gov/MedicareEligibility).

Enrollment in Medicare is through the Social Security Administration. Contact your local Social Security Office or call:

- Social Security: 800-772-1213.
- TTY users: 800-325-0778.
- Railroad Retirement Board: 800-808-0772.

Each December, Medicare publishes the handbook, *Medicare and You*, which describes the Medicare program specifics for the coming year. Call or visit the Medicare website to obtain a copy of the publication:

- Medicare: 800-633-4227.
- TTY users: 877-486-2048.
- Medicare website: www.medicare.gov.

The Social Security Administration recommends that you sign up for Medicare when you become eligible at age 65 or receive Social Security disability benefits.

> *IMPORTANT: as soon as you are no longer covered by an employer's medical plan and are at least 65*

years of age, you should enroll in Medicare Part B coverage to avoid any premium penalty.

Your decision on whether or not to participate in Medicare Part B is critical. If you do not join when you are first eligible, and then join at a later time, there will be a 10% premium penalty *added for each year* that you did not join. There is an exception to the imposition of the penalty: if you are 65, still working and covered by an employer's insurance plan, you do not have to enroll in Part B until you quit working.

Military retirees, at age 65, have TRICARE for Life medical coverage and are also required to enroll in Medicare Part B.

The Parts of Medicare

No self-respecting government program would make the details of its purpose clear for anyone who doesn't speak government-ese, but Medicare has made a decent effort to clearly present the details of the program. Let's break this down by "Parts," the way Medicare is structured.

There are currently four parts to the program - Parts A, B, D, and Medicare Advantage Plans.

Part A - Hospital Insurance:

- Covers inpatient care in hospitals, skilled nursing facilities after a hospital stay, hospice, and some home health care.
- Starts automatically at age 65.
- Most people don't pay for this coverage (if you have worked at least 10 years in Medicare-covered

employment).

- Does not cover long-term care or custodial care.
- You pay some fee-for-service costs such as copayments, and deductibles. These are known as Medicare gaps.
- Check the Medicare web site for additional details (www.medicare.gov).

Part B - Medical Insurance:

- Optional coverage. A monthly premium is charged if you choose to enroll. If you don't join when **you are first eligible** at age 65, the premium increases 10% for each year that you did not join! At age 65 if you are still working **and** covered by a health plan, you may defer enrolling in Part B until you retire without incurring this penalty.
- Covers doctors, outpatient hospital, and some other medical services. You may still have some out-of-pocket copayment expenses.
- Premium increases if your income exceeds certain levels: $85,000 if single; $170,000 if joint return (for the year 2011).
- You have eight months to enroll after you turn 65 or your employment ends. Delaying enrollment after that period will incur a permanent 10% per year premium penalty.
- General Enrollment Period is January 1 through March 31 of each year.
- A Special Enrollment Period, available only to those who were employed and covered by an employer health plan when they turned 65, is a one-time eight-month period immediately following the end of employment.

Part D - Prescription Drug Plan (PDP):

- You are eligible if you participate in Medicare Part A or Part B.
- Join a private prescription drug plan or Medicare Advantage Plan.
- Costs and coverages are not standardized; each plan decides which drugs to cover.
- Cost of the plan (premiums and deductibles) varies by the plan you choose.
- Cost of drugs is usually less, but you may still pay a copayment or deductible.
- Individuals with limited income or resources may qualify for cost assistance.

So what happened to Part C? The Medicare administrator prefers the term Medicare Advantage Plans when referring to what should have been called Part C. These are plans approved by Medicare and run by private companies such as insurance companies or medical groups. Medicare also refers to these plans as Medicare Health Plans.

Medicare Advantage Plans.

- A Medicare Health Plan offered by
  - Medicare Health Maintenance Organizations (HMOs)
  - Preferred Provider Organizations (PPOs)
  - Private fee-for-service plans
  - Medicare Special Needs plans
  - Various Provider Sponsored Organizations (PSOs).

- You must participate in Medicare Part A and Part B.
- You may be required to use a doctor or hospital that participates in the plan.
- Out-of pocket costs may be lower.
- You may pay a copayment and deductible.
- May include prescription drug coverage.
- Additional monthly premiums may be imposed for additional coverages.

Participation in the Part D - Prescription Drug Program and a Medicare Advantage Plan is optional. You may make changes in a plan once a year, usually from mid-November through the end of the year.

Out-of-Pocket Expenses and Premiums

Have you ever tried to help someone determine their responsibility for a medical expense and to understand what portion of the expense Medicare will cover? Or have you tried to determine the cost for certain Medicare covered services? I have, and it wasn't an easy task. At the time, I didn't know what was covered or how much was deductible. Being a list person, I was lost without a list of coverages and costs.

The following is a list of premiums, deductibles, and coinsurance for the various Medicare parts:

Premiums for 2011

The premiums are subject to change each January 1. Check the Medicare web site for the latest premiums, deductibles, and copayments: www.medicare.gov/spotlights.asp.

Part A - Hospital Insurance

No cost for persons with 40 months of covered Medicare-taxable employment. There is a monthly premium if you have less than the 40 months of covered employment; i.e., less than 40 months of paying the Medicare tax on your wages. With 30-39 months of covered employment, the cost is $244 a month. With less than 30 months of covered employment, the cost is $461 a month.

Part B - Medical Insurance

$110.50 a month for the year 2011 if your annual income is less than $170,000 (Joint) or $85,000 (Individual). For higher incomes the monthly premium can range up to $353.60.

Part D - Prescription Drug Plan

The costs will vary depending upon the particular Prescription Drug Plan you select. You may be eligible for assistance with the plan costs if you have limited income and resources.

Medicare Advantage Plans

These Medicare approved plans are run by private insurance companies or medical organizations, and the premiums vary depending upon the plan selected. Typically you may be required to use a physician or hospital that is in the plan, therefore your out-of-pocket costs may be lower.

Deductibles and Coinsurance for 2011

Part A - Inpatient Hospital Care, Skilled Nursing Facility and Some Home Health Care.

Hospital - *you pay:*

First 60 days: a total deductible of $1,100

61-90 days: $275 per day

91-150 days: $550 per day

Beyond 150 days: all costs

Skilled nursing facility - *you pay:*

First 20 days: no additional cost to you

21-100 days: $137.50 per day

Beyond 100 days: all costs

Part B - Eligible Physician Services, Outpatient Hospital Services, Some Home Health Care and Durable Medical Equipment.

You pay the first $155 (annual deductible), then 20% of the Medicare-approved amount for services.

Part D - Prescription Drug Plans.

The deductible and monthly premium will vary by plan. Be sure you understand which drugs are covered, the annual deductible, and the monthly premium before signing up.

Medicare Supplemental Insurance

Medicare Supplemental Insurance policies help pay your out-of-pocket costs not covered by Medicare. These policies are sold by insurance companies and are known as "Medigap" policies. If you select a Medicare Advantage health plan, a supplemental insurance plan is usually a duplication of coverages and is not necessary. These policies are not cheap. Obviously the more coverage for reimbursement that you choose, the greater the monthly premium. Some of the expenses covered by the supplemental policies include:

- Part A and Part B excess charges.
- Foreign travel emergencies.
- Preventive care.
- At-home recovery.
- Skilled nursing facilities.

Chapter Questions

1. What is Medicare? Who collects and accounts for the Medicare premiums?

2. What are the Parts of Medicare?

3. What determines someone's eligibility for Medicare?

4. What medical expenses does each Part cover?

5. When should someone sign up for Part B participation?

6. Are there any copayments or deductibles for Part A coverage?

7. Are there any copayments or deductibles for Part B coverage?

8. What does Medicare Part D cover?

9. What is a Medicare Advantage Plan, and what services does it pay for?

10. What does Medicare Part B cost? Where can you find the cost for income levels for the current year?

Chapter 18
Managing Your Retirement Accounts

Chapter Objectives

- Understand your responsibilities with retirement accounts.
- Group retirement accounts into passive or managed groups.
- See your total investment portfolio as one unit.
- Understand the role of rebalancing your portfolio.
- Know what a target-date or life-cycle fund provides.

Retirement accounts come in several shapes, sizes, predictabilities, and options. The best approach for managing these various sources of retirement income is to view them in total, as one portfolio. Understanding how your retirement accounts work together in harmony will help you maintain your appropriate asset allocation. Your asset allocation should be seen for the total portfolio, not individual accounts. Some accounts or retirement plans may be more heavily skewed toward equities or bonds than another account. What's important is to keep your total portfolio balanced to your asset allocation.

Sources of Retirement Income

Before jumping into the management of your retirement accounts, let's review where your retirement income will come from. Begin by making a list of your potential sources of income. To get the list started, consider the following:

- Social Security.
- Employer pension (defined-benefit plan).
- Employer-sponsored retirement plan (defined-contribution: 401(k), 403(b), etc.).
- Military, teachers, or union retirement plan.
- IRAs.
- Personal savings and investments not in a retirement plan.
- Fixed annuity.
- Other sources of a steady stream of income.

While this list covers most of our possible sources, your particular retirement circumstances may provide for other sources of income. Do you have any employment from the distant past which might have earned you a vested retirement income? If you are unsure, contact previous employers and check it out. Retirement is no time to leave any money on the table.

Understanding Active and Passive Management

For a clearer understanding of what's involved in dealing with the various sources of retirement income, divide your income into two groups. In one group are the passive income sources—you are a passive recipient with no responsibilities for managing the plan. In the second group are your savings and investments for which you are responsible for the active management and oversight, such as an IRA, 401(k), brokerage accounts, or CDs.

Division of responsibility for oversight and management:

- Passive - your role is recipient only
  - Social Security.
  - Employer-sponsored defined-benefit plan.
  - Military, teachers or union retirement plan.
  - Fixed annuity.
- Active - your role is managing and choosing asset classes or investments
  - IRA.
  - Employer-sponsored defined-contribution plan.
  - 401(k), 403(b), 457, SEP IRA, etc.
  - Personal savings and investments not in retirement plans; e.g., stocks, bonds, mutual funds, ETFs, CD's, savings and money market accounts.

Add any other source of income to the above groups that would be applicable to your situation.

It's a no-brainer to be the passive recipient of some sources of income such as Social Security or a company pension. All you need to do is sit back and receive the monthly check. You cannot make any decision regarding how the assets of the retirement plan are invested.

However, it is your responsibility for the management and investment decisions of your self-directed accounts. These accounts include your IRAs, employer defined-contribution retirement plans with mutual fund choices (401(k)), savings, and any other investments not in a managed account. It is your responsibility to keep the savings and investments in these accounts in sync with your desired asset allocation. A goal for this book is to help you with those decisions.

Rebalancing Your Portfolio

To keep your portfolio in line with your desired asset allocation, you will need to periodically rebalance the portfolio. Rebalancing involves buying or selling investments in one asset class in order to bring that class of asset back to its desired allocation. For example, if equities have risen to 48% of your portfolio, but you want equities to be 40%, you must sell equities equal to 8% of the portfolio and buy assets in another class which is below its desired allocation.

Rebalancing your investments will help you to stay on track with your investment plan. It's a correcting process that moves money into asset classes which have declined and takes money out of an asset class that has increased in value since the last rebalancing. During a stock market advance when equities have risen, rebalancing takes money out of stocks and places it into the more stable fixed income class. This will help you capture some of the gains you may have made in equities during the advance. Rebalancing is also helpful during stock market lows when it's prudent to take money out of fixed income assets and increase your investment in equities.

> *An annual review and rebalancing of your portfolio, will reduce your chances of reacting emotionally during market highs and lows or trying to "time the market." Rebalancing more frequently than once a year can negatively impact your portfolio during prolonged down markets.*

To determine the asset allocation for a mutual fund, use the latest report from the mutual fund or go to the fund company's web site. Many funds may hold assets which overlap asset classes. For example, a domestic equity stock fund may also have investments in foreign equities. Balanced funds will be invested in both equities and fixed income securities. Taking the time to determine the fund's or ETF's allocation percentages will help you to more accurately maintain your asset allocation.

To determine your current asset allocation and rebalance your total portfolio, use Table D-4, Personal Asset Allocation & Investment Category worksheet (Appendix D). Before you begin, review the instructions and the example of a completed worksheet which follow Table D-5B. Also, review Chapter 12 for additional details on the rebalancing procedure.

Autopilot - Using Target-Date Funds

Some folks may find the rebalancing process too involved for their level of commitment to managing their investments. If you are one of those, relax; the financial community has developed a product just for you. It's the "autopilot" approach—someone else does the rebalancing for you.

A number of mutual fund companies have developed a series of funds that will self-adjust the asset allocation among classes, as a future date approaches. These funds may include "life-cycle" or "target-date" in the fund name or description. A future date or number of years, such as 2015, 2020, or 20 Year, may also be part of the fund name. Some examples are Vanguard Target Retirement 2015 Fund, L 2030 Fund, Freedom Fund 2025, or USAA Target Retirement 2020 Fund.

The main attraction of these funds is the automatic adjustment of the asset allocation between equities and fixed income as the target date approaches. For example, a fund targeted to mature in 2030, may start out with an asset allocation of 70% equities and 30% fixed income. Then every 5 years or so, it will become more conservative in its allocation and move a portion of the assets out of equities and into fixed income. These target-date funds are typically composed of stock and bond funds from the same fund family.

The following example demonstrates how funds become more conservative, by reducing their equity allocation, as they move closer to their target date.

Example of some target-date fund allocations:

Fund	Equities	Fixed Income
2015 Fund	40 %	60 %
2020 Fund	50 %	50 %
2025 Fund	60 %	40 %

If you find that the annual rebalancing of your investment assets is more than you can deal with, consider using target-date funds to achieve your asset allocation and rebalancing goals.

If you use target-date funds for your investments, keep in mind that the asset allocations will vary among the various funds and fund companies in spite of their similar targeted dates. One fund may implement a more aggressive allocation—equity oriented—than another fund with the same target date. I suggest you determine your asset allocation first, then find a target-date fund that most closely fits your allocation and comfort range.

A word of caution: during the stock market crash of 2008/2009, the losses in target-date funds were quite divergent. A target-date fund will not protect you from market crashes. These funds will experience the same fluctuations as any portfolio with matching asset allocations. Funds with significant allocations to equities were down as much as 40% or more in 2008/2009. Some with a greater allocation toward fixed income had smaller losses. The primary determinant was their asset allocation, not a targeted date. Be sure to check the fund's portfolio allocation for a close match to your desired allocation before investing.

Chapter Questions

1. What are the two groups into which the sources of retirement income may be divided?

2. List your sources of retirement income which (will) fall into the passive management group.

3. List your sources of retirement income which (will) fall into the active management group.

4. How frequently should you review and rebalance your investment portfolio? Are you comfortable with the time interval suggested for rebalancing? Why do you feel that way?

5. What common investor mistake can be lessened with an annual rebalancing of assets?

6. What does rebalancing your assets involve?

7. What is the primary characteristic of a target-date mutual fund?

8. If your desired asset allocation is -

    Equities - 40%

    Fixed Income - 50%

    Cash Equivalents - 10%

    and your portfolio has the following funds with current values -

Equity Fund A	$20,000
Equity Fund B	15,000
Bond Fund C	60,000
Money Market Fund	5,000

    What asset class(s) is over its desired goal? By how much?

    What asset class(s) is under its desired goal? By how much?

    What fund(s) would you sell and how much?

    What fund(s) would you buy and how much?

Chapter 19
Establishing a Withdrawal Plan

Chapter Objectives

- Understand the impact of inflation.
- Use a retirement budget to prepare monthly withdrawal amount.
- Set a withdrawal rate you can live with.
- See the impact of a withdrawal rate on your retirement portfolio.
- Understand different withdrawal concepts.
- Know withdrawal priorities for different accounts.
- Understand tax implications for retirement accounts.

The Impact of Inflation and Consumer Price Index

As retirement kicks in, so will the gradual affects of inflation. The expenses you can handle today may become a real challenge tomorrow. The villain here is compounding. The same mathematical advantage you get from compound interest is now working against you by compounding the affects of inflation on your expenses.

I wish there were an easier way to break the news about inflation; but what is, is. Before you get into a dark funk, here is some encouragement on the inflation front. Some of your sources of retirement income will also increase each year to help you keep up with the impact of inflation. Social Security payments rise with, or are close to, the rate of inflation as measured by the consumer price index (CPI-W).[25] Some employer-sponsored retirement plans may also be pegged to inflation or the CPI.

Therefore, whether you are still working and accumulating assets for retirement, or you have retired, it's important to have an asset allocation that keeps a portion of your portfolio invested in equities. Over the long-term, nothing has helped the investor overcome the affects of inflation better than equities.

Recall the second half of 2008, when the stock market declined over 25% in a matter of six weeks and then plunged an additional 15% in one week in October. A 40% decline in your investments does not generate confidence in an investment plan which includes equities. Our emotions are screaming, "Get out!" But as the economic decline slows and eventually recovers, no asset class offers a better potential than equities. If you understand that no one can consistently time the market, and that equity investments offer the best opportunity to help you stay ahead of inflation, then your only option is to keep some portion of your portfolio invested in equities, during both the up and down cycles of the market.

With proper portfolio asset allocation, periodic rebalancing, and implementation of a prudent withdrawal plan, you will be able to ride out the inevitable bear markets. That is the key to a successful retirement plan for your retirement years.

I hope you find it encouraging to know that a broad stock market investment portfolio has over the last 30 years increased at an annualized rate of 10.3%. Fixed income investments during that period have returned from 2.5% to 6%, depending upon the type of underlying bond portfolio and level of risk. High-risk junk bonds have provided higher returns, but they come with a level of risk most retirees should avoid.

How Much Should You Withdraw Each Year?

Let's turn our focus to the issue of withdrawing funds from our investment portfolio during retirement. The critical question is, "How much should I take out of my savings and investments each year to live on?"

Before you can answer that question, complete the following:

- Develop a retirement budget.
- Determine the amount of Social Security and other pensions you will receive monthly.
- Establish an asset allocation for retirement with which you are comfortable.
- Resolve the issue of leaving an inheritance.
- Identify areas of your lifestyle where spending adjustments could be made if necessary to accommodate your level of income.

Armed with that information, you are now aware of your anticipated retirement expenses, the amount of Social Security and other pension income you will be receiving, and of any possible shortage of income that would leave some of your anticipated expenses uncovered. If Social Security and pension income covers your anticipated expenses, you can leave your savings and investments untouched until you reach 70½ when you will be required to take withdrawals from IRAs or 401(k)s. If that is you,

you are in a very fortunate minority. But continue to review and rebalance your investment portfolio annually in order to maintain your asset allocation.

For the rest of us, we will need to withdraw funds from savings and investments to supplement our monthly retirement income. So back to the question: "How much should I take out of my savings and investments each year to live on?"

There is an unmentioned issue behind that question—the fear of outliving our financial resources. The thought of living out our final years in poverty is not pleasant or an issue we speak of often, certainly not as frequently as we may privately ponder the possibility.

It has been my experience that clients who mentioned this worry were more likely to leave my office and drive home in a fairly new Buick, Cadillac, Lexus, or Grand Marquis than in a 9-year-old Junker. Over the years their level of income had afforded them comfort, and they rarely lacked the means to satisfy their wants. Now, in retirement, they were dealing with the reality of income, needs, and wants. Some fretted over how they would maintain a lifestyle they had become accustomed to during their working years.

However, one memorable friend, an elderly woman who had to take public transportation most of the time because her 9-year-old car was "down again," never mentioned that concern or gave it a thought. That is a peace you won't get from your portfolio, no matter how large it is.

So here is the reality. You can withdraw between 4% and 6% annually from your savings and investments and have some probability of not out-living your savings.

Obviously, the smaller the withdrawal rate, the longer your savings will last. The withdrawal issue involves with both your finances and your emotions. What rate of withdrawal can you live with—materially and emotionally?

This chart will help put this in some perspective:

Rate of Withdrawal Annually	**Probability of NOT Outliving Your Savings for 30 Years**
4%	90%
5%	75%
6%	40%

This chart reflects a Monte Carlo simulation of numerous scenarios for a 30-year duration of an investment portfolio with a 60% equities/40% fixed income mix.

There is only one withdrawal rate which I can honestly recommend to you—the 4% annual withdrawal. Anything above a 4% withdrawal rate introduces a level of uncertainty which most people find uncomfortable.

Of course individual circumstances such as age, health, and family responsibilities should influence your decision, but for most of us who will face this decision in our mid-60's, a 4% rate is usually sustainable and emotionally comfortable.

Withdrawal Rate Variations

There are two popular variations for withdrawing funds from your retirement accounts:

- Dollar-adjusted withdrawal: determine a withdrawal amount the first year, then adjust the amount each year after that for inflation.
- Percentage withdrawal: calculate a withdrawal amount as a fixed percentage of the portfolio each year with no adjustment for inflation.

A withdrawal based on a dollar-adjusted formula will increase your withdrawal each year by the percentage of inflation. The withdrawal the first year is calculated by applying a withdrawal percentage to your portfolio at the first year of retirement. A certain dollar amount is calculated. Then beginning with the second and subsequent years, increase the withdrawal by the annual rate of inflation.

> For example, a $400,000 portfolio with a withdrawal rate of 4% will provide $16,000 the first year. Then, the next year if the inflation rate is 3%, increase the withdrawal by 3% of the $16,000. The withdrawal amount the second year is $16,480. The next year if inflation goes to 4%, add 4% of the $16,480 to the withdrawal, for a total withdrawal of $17,139. Repeat this calculation each year.

A withdrawal based on a percentage withdrawal uses a fixed percentage each year regardless of the rate of inflation. This rate is applied to the total value of the portfolio regardless of market ups or downs. During bear markets, when the value of your portfolio declines, the dollar amount of the withdrawal will also decline. This method can help keep you from consuming all your retirement savings/investments, since it is based on a percentage of the current portfolio value.

> For example, a $500,000 portfolio with a withdrawal percentage of 4% would provide $20,000 for the year.

Keep in mind that flexibility can be a real advantage when setting your withdrawal. Start with one of these two approaches; if you find it too cumbersome, switch to the other. The critical decision here is to select an initial withdrawal rate that will achieve your goal of not out-living your savings while providing money to meet retirement expenses.

Withdrawing from Which Account?

As I have previously mentioned, you should view the total of your investments as one portfolio. To determine the value of your portfolio, add the current market value of all your savings and investment accounts. Deal with them as one portfolio when setting your asset allocation and withdrawals. You may choose to withdraw from one account over another for convenience or because one account has more cash sitting around, but view them in total as one portfolio for planning purposes.

Different types of accounts will require different withdrawal patterns. For example, a traditional IRA will be treated differently than a Roth IRA. There is no required withdrawal from a Roth

IRA; the account may remain untouched during your lifetime and passed on to the designated beneficiary(s). However, the traditional IRA requires that withdrawals begin at least by the time you reach 70½, but not before 59½ to avoid a penalty.

A 401(k) account also requires that withdrawals start at least by 70½.

Keep track of the amount of your retirement account withdrawals in order to know if withdrawals late in the year might push you into a higher tax bracket. If you use an accountant, ask where you stand tax-wise. If you need a withdrawal late in the year, and the amount would push your income into the next higher tax bracket, withdraw the funds from a tax-free account such as a Roth IRA or Roth 401(k) instead of a tax-deferred account such as a traditional IRA or a 401(k). To avoid a tax penalty, be sure you are withdrawing the required minimums from your tax-deferred accounts.

If you are fortunate enough to have several different types of accounts, withdraw from the accounts in the following order until the desired annual withdrawal amount is reached:

1. Income from taxable non-retirement accounts: money market, maturing CDs, brokerage account dividends and interest.
2. Tax-deferred retirement accounts: traditional IRA, 401(k), 403(b), SEP IRA, etc.
3. Tax-free retirement accounts: Roth IRA, Roth 401(k).

Once you reach 70½, alter the order to accommodate the required withdrawals:

1. Tax-deferred retirement accounts which require minimum distributions: traditional IRA, 401(k), Roth 401(k), 403(b), SEP IRA, etc.
2. Income from taxable non-retirement accounts: money market, maturing CDs, brokerage account dividends and interest.
3. Tax-free retirement account: Roth IRA.

Note on the above withdrawal recommendations: As you withdraw from savings, money market accounts, and maturing CDs, be sure that you maintain the cash equivalent level of your asset allocation. In retirement, your cash equivalents should be at least 10% of your total portfolio. See Chapter 7, Asset Allocation, for more information. Also note that one withdrawal plan can't fit all possible situations. If you are unsure of the tax consequences of your withdrawals, consult your accountant for tax guidance.

To generate the cash needed for withdrawal from the various investment accounts, you will need to occasionally sell some investments. Keep your asset allocation in mind as you sell equities and fixed income securities. Don't let the selling process get your asset allocation off your goal.

Again, let me repeat: Don't try to time the market. Sell and rebalance your portfolio at established times during the year. Keep in mind your anticipated cash needs during the coming year as you rebalance your portfolio.

If you have mutual fund accounts, consider establishing a periodic withdrawal from the account. This can be arranged through the mutual fund company or brokerage firm. Check with the firm for details of their withdrawal programs, minimums, fees, and options.

As you step into retirement and are ready to begin withdrawing funds from your retirement accounts, you can greatly simplify the withdrawal process by *consolidating traditional IRAs into one traditional IRA account at one brokerage firm, mutual fund company, or bank,* instead of keeping the accounts spread out among different firms. If you decide to consolidate accounts, keep in mind that you will not be able to combine tax-deferred accounts (traditional IRA) and tax-free accounts (Roth IRA) into one account.

Withdrawal of Securities

There is another twist on the withdrawal process. Once you begin to make withdrawals from your IRA, consider a withdrawal of shares of stock or mutual funds instead of selling the security and withdrawing the cash. This can be helpful if you don't need cash from the IRA and want to continue owning the stock or mutual fund.

You or your broker will still need to determine the dollar amount of the required withdrawal. But instead of taking cash, transfer shares equal in value to the required withdrawal amount into a taxable account. For tax purposes, the event still has a reportable dollar value, but you still own the shares and have saved the commissions on the sale and repurchase of the security.

Your new cost basis for the security is the value of the shares on the day they were transferred. The transfer date is also used to determine a short-term or long-term holding period when you eventually sell the security from the taxable account.

Check with your brokerage firm to see if they have any rules prohibiting this type of transfer. The transfer should be between accounts at one firm, since transferring to a taxable account at another firm will most likely trigger a transfer charge, making this type of withdrawal too expensive to be useful.

Withdrawals and Taxes

Uncle Sam doesn't give you a free ride forever. Sooner or later, the taxman wants the taxes due on the deferred income accounts—your traditional IRA, 401(k), 403(b), etc. All of your contributions that were tax deductible are now taxable income when withdrawn. Once you reach 70½ you must begin to take withdrawals from those accounts and pay the taxes at your current year tax rate.

Let me break this down starting with the most straightforward principle first. Contributions you made to your 401(k), 403(b), or any tax-deferred retirement plan reduced your taxable income by the amount of the contribution in the year you made the contribution. Now the tax is due. You must pay taxes at your current tax rate on all the money that is withdrawn from these accounts.

With the traditional IRA, your contributions may have been either tax-deductible or non-deductible. Depending upon your income level and participation in an employer-sponsored retirement or pension plan during the year of the contribution, you may have deducted the contribution from your income. See Form 8606 from your federal income tax return for the cumulative amount of non-deductible contributions to your traditional IRA.

The non-deductible portion of withdrawals from your traditional IRA will not be taxed; you have already paid tax on that money. However, you will pay tax on the tax deductible contributions which you made and on all accumulated earnings.

Tax Treatment of Traditional IRA Contributions/Earnings		
Contribution was:	In past years	At withdrawal
Non-deductible	Taxed	Not taxed
Deductible	Tax-deferred	Taxable
All earnings are:	Tax-deferred	Taxable

The Roth IRA affords several advantages over the traditional IRA. When the account has been opened for at least five years, the growth and earnings are tax-free, not just tax-deferred. There is also no requirement for withdrawals when you reach 70½. See Chapter 12 for additional information on IRAs.

Chapter Questions

1. What impact does inflation have on your retirement income?

2. List your retirement accounts which will have an automatic cost-of-living adjustment.

3. What is the recommended withdrawal rate from your savings and investments that will provide a 90% probably that you will not out-live your assets?

4. Why is it usually advantageous to withdraw retirement income from other accounts before withdrawing funds from a Roth IRA? When can it be advantageous to withdraw from a Roth IRA?

5. With a traditional IRA…
   - Is the full amount of the withdrawal always taxable?
   - How would you determine your non-deductible portion of the withdrawal?
   - Are some earnings in the IRA non-taxable on withdrawal?

Chapter 20
What about Annuities?

Chapter Objectives

- Learn the characteristics of annuities.
- Know the difference between fixed and variable annuities.
- Understand the proper role of a fixed annuity.
- Understand the abuses and problems with annuities.

One of the most challenging investment decisions you will make is whether or not to use an annuity in your retirement planning. If you rely on the barrage of advertising, which we are subjected to almost daily, you may be mislead or confused about annuities—what annuities are, how to incorporate one into your planning, or even whether you should use an annuity at all.

> As a point of full disclosure, during my active years in the financial services business, in addition to my securities licenses, I also had an insurance license and sold annuities.

In the last few years, we have been deluged with sales pitches which offer *guaranteed* retirement income for life. The ads usually play on our fear of outliving our money or losing our retirement nest egg in a stock market collapse. Often the ads pitch a high rate of return (a "teaser rate") or the guarantee of income and upside potential ("stock market gains without the downside risk").

Oh, really? How is this possible? If you examine more closely this "high-potential, no-risk" investment, it turns out to be an annuity. In many cases, the salesperson will not mention the word *annuity* for fear the prospect may actually read a newspaper or has otherwise heard of annuity abuses.

The guarantee which the annuity offers is only as good as the ability of the insurance company to meet its obligations to the annuity owner. They will use hedging strategies in the stock and bond markets to meet the obligations they promise to annuity owners—the expectation of the promised *guaranteed* income.

Insurance companies must also meet regulatory capital requirements. As the financial crisis of 2008-2009 unfolded, a few insurance companies ran into trouble. Some large insurers converted themselves into banks in order to qualify for the Troubled Asset Relief Program. Their capital bases had deteriorated significantly in the stock market collapse. The Wall Street Journal reported that one large insurer asked regulators to ease the capital requirement (capital set aside to meet policyholder/annuity owner claims). The Journal explained that the recent "market downdraft has ratcheted up the liability, in particular, of big sellers of guaranteed-minimum retirement-income products known as variable annuities."[26]

In early 2009 as the stock and bond markets continued to fall, a few state insurance regulators eased a requirement for some of the largest insurers, that they put up additional capital to meet their obligations to policyholders. In March of 2009, a Wall Street Journal headline read "Worry Grows Over Insurers As Ratings Slip."[27] The article pointed out problems large and small insurers are having with bad investments and questions about their ability to meet future claims from various policyholders including annuities. The variable annuities which life insurance companies offer consumers "pay a guaranteed return, regardless of whether bulls or bears are running the stock market. [These future obligations are forcing these insurance companies] into protective strategies that make it hard to offset the risks they've assumed."[28]

I won't mince words. With one exception, you should not use an annuity in your retirement planning—either before or during retirement.

That exception is the purchase of an immediate fixed annuity for a steady stream of income that you will not outlive. Before I explain this particular variety of annuity and how you might utilize it in your retirement planning, let me define annuities, their uses and abuses, and why most annuities are sold on an emotional basis and not as a supplemental source of income for retirement.

Visit the Securities and Exchange Commission's web site, www.sec.gov/investor/pubs/varannty.htm, for additional details concerning annuities. The site provides definitions and what questions you should ask before purchasing an annuity.

What is an Annuity?

An annuity is an insurance contract packaged and sold by an insurance company. You purchase an annuity with either an initial deposit (the purchase amount) or periodic investments into the annuity. The earnings on the annuity are tax-deferred during the *accumulation phase*—this is the period when the annuity may grow in value. The *payout phase* is the period during which you receive periodic payments, usually monthly. These payments will include both a return of your principal (original investment) and earnings on the principal. The return of principal portion of the payout is tax free, and the earnings portion of the payout is taxable at your current tax rate.

Annuities are also identified by their accumulation (growth) phase.

> An *immediate annuity* has no accumulation phase. The payout phase begins immediately after you make your annuity purchase (deposit).
>
> A *deferred annuity* has an accumulation phase where your investment(s) will increase at (1) a stated rate, (2) at a rate equal to an investment index, or (3) by the performance of a mutual fund(s) portfolio.

Insurance companies impose numerous charges and expenses against the value of the annuity contract. Annuity charges and fees may include the following:

> Surrender charges - a penalty imposed if you cancel and surrender the contract within a few years after purchase. This period can be five years or longer—sometimes as long as 10 years. Usually the surrender charge is reduced over time. This charge can be quite burdensome as some surrender charges may be 5% or more of your initial purchase. Some annuity contracts will allow you to withdraw a percentage of the annuity value each year without a penalty. Once you start the

payout phase, called annuitization of the contract, it is usually not possible to surrender the annuity back to the insurance company.

Mortality and expense risk charge - a percentage of the value of the annuity is charged each year to compensate for the uncertainties (risk) of mortality on the individual owning the annuity and the costs to provide a guaranteed payout. Typically this charge may be 1.25%.

Mutual fund fees - variable annuities which offer mutual fund investment options will additionally impose fund management expenses.

Administrative fees - to compensate for record-keeping and other expenses of administering and maintaining the annuity. This may be a flat fee or a percentage of the annuity value.

Sales charge or load - compensation to the salesperson. Sometimes this may not be evident or listed as a separate charge, but the salesperson is compensated by the insurance company.

Guaranteed benefits - you may choose add-on guarantees such as minimum income or minimum withdrawal benefits. The annual charge for this guarantee is typically an additional 0.5% - 1.0%. The charge for index-linked annuities can be as high as 3%.

Various other charges - depending upon the features or exotic nature of the variable annuity, such as guaranteed minimum income benefit or stepped-up death benefit, other charges may be imposed.

Types of Annuities

There are two types of annuities: fixed and variable.

Fixed Annuity –

A fixed annuity is an insurance contract that guarantees you a minimum return on your purchase: a fixed rate of interest, a fixed dollar amount, or another amount using a formula. The performance is not dependent upon any variable or investment; the return is fixed.

A fixed annuity may be either an immediate annuity or deferred annuity with a future payout phase. A fixed annuity can provide periodic payments for the rest of your life or jointly with the life of another person, such as a spouse. This is the strongest selling point for annuities: a periodic payment for life, a source of income you cannot out live. You may also take the value of the annuity contract as one lump sum payment. See payout options below.

Some fixed annuities have recently morphed to attract purchasers who want some variety or greater potential return by offering "equity-indexed" annuities or "market-value-adjusted" annuities. These offer you an adjustment on the value of the annuity based on an underlying equity index. These are really variable-annuities in a fixed annuity wrapper.

Variable Annuity -

A variable annuity is an insurance contract which offers a variety of investment options. The value of the annuity and its subsequent payout potential will vary or fluctuate depending upon the performance of the chosen investment option during the accumulation phase. Variable annuities are sold to include investment choices such as stock indices or mutual funds, bond indices or mutual funds, interest rates, etc. These investment choices are known as sub-accounts within the annuity.

In the payout phase, the variable annuity will provide periodic payments for the rest of your life or the life of another person. You may also take the value of the annuity contract as one lump sum payment. Be careful with a lump sum payment; the tax is levied on the full increased value of the contract in the year you receive the payment instead of being spread out over many years.

Variable annuities can also include a death benefit for your beneficiary, which guarantees that the beneficiary would receive a specified amount, usually no less than your original purchase less any withdrawals.

Variable annuities are either an *immediate annuity* with the payout phase starting immediately after the purchase, or a *deferred annuity* with a payout phase starting at some date in the future.

Annuity Payout Choices

A critical decision for all annuity owners (annuitants) is the choice of payout option for the payout phase. When the accumulation phase ends and the payout phase begins, the annuitant begins to receive income payments from the annuity for life or a specific number of years. The transition of the annuity from the accumulation phase into the payout phase is called annuitization—converting the value of the annuity into a stream of periodic payments.

The payments are calculated using the value of the annuity at the time of annuitization. With the annuitization method, you are choosing to receive the value of the annuity as either a stream of periodic payments, or as a lump sum. As I previously mentioned, understand that the lump sum choice will mean that the tax on the appreciated value of the annuity is due in the year you receive the lump sum payment. Usually this is not a good choice of payouts.

Another option for taking money out of an annuity is called systematic withdrawals. This method lets the owner choose a payment amount and take withdrawals until the value of the annuity is zero. With this method there is no annuitization; therefore, no guarantee of income for life.

Payment choices for the payout phase:

- Stream of payments over a specified period:
  - Lifetime of owner.
  - Lifetime of owner and another person.
  - Period Certain (5, 10, 15, 20... years).

  - Lifetime with a specific term.
  - Lifetime with remaining lump sum to beneficiary.
- Lump sum payment.
- Longevity rider.

Some annuities may offer other payout choices. Usually the more exotic the underlying investment, the more exotic the payout options and the higher the annuity expenses.

Unless the value of the annuity is very small or will not significantly impact your current year taxes, the choice of a stream of payments is better than the lump sum payment. Check with your tax advisor for guidance on your specific tax situation.

> *Note: the longer the payout phase or greater the guarantee(s), the smaller the periodic payment will be. You are asking the insurance company to assume a greater risk; i.e., the insurance company will be paying you for a longer period or is guaranteeing you or your beneficiaries a minimum payout.*

Be careful when choosing a payout method. If you choose the option of *lifetime of the annuitant only*, without a lump sum to a beneficiary, *the payout phase is over at your death*. There will be no more payments to anyone even if your death was shortly after you begun receiving payments.

I can hear you asking, "Why would anyone choose the lifetime of the owner only?" I can only assume it's because the amount of the periodic payment will be larger, and they are willing to take the chance for a larger payment today. Trust me; the insurance companies have this figured out. They know statistically how long you, as a member of a group of annuitants, are going to live. They are not taking a risk. You and your heirs are assuming the risk of not receiving the full value of the annuity in exchange for a larger periodic payment until your death. Obviously, this is not a recommended option.

The *Period Certain choice, also known as specific term or fixed period*, will provide you a payout for your lifetime. If you die before the end of the period certain, the designated beneficiary will continue to receive the payment for the remainder of the period. Typically, you may select a period from 5 to 30 years.

A *joint and survivor life annuity with a period certain or fixed period* will provide a payout for the lifetime of the annuitant. If the annuitant dies first, before the end of the period certain, the payout continues until the end of the period certain, then the survivor receives a reduced payout (50-100%) depending upon the contract, for the rest of his/her life. If both die before the end of the fixed period, the beneficiary will receive the monthly payments for the remainder of the period selected.

When the insurance company calculates the payout amount, it factors in the additional guarantees, not just the current value of the annuity. The annuity with a lifetime payout and a lump sum to a beneficiary increases the potential payout liability for the insurance company. Therefore, the payment will be smaller than if the payout was only for a specific number of years (period certain).

The *Longevity Rider* is another option available from most insurance companies. This essentially is an annuity which does not start paying until age 75, 80, or later. Its purpose is to provide you with a guaranteed income starting much later in life. With a guaranteed death benefit, these policies can also provide some payout to your heirs. When you utilize annuities with longevity riders, this extra long-range protection can allow you to take on more risk with your other investments. That is, you may allocate more of your total investment portfolio to equities—depending upon your risk tolerance—during your earlier years of retirement.

Variable Annuity Concerns

As I said, except for the immediate fixed annuity, I do not recommend annuities as part of a retirement plan. Here is a brief list of the reasons why I believe you should avoid variable annuities:

- They are very expensive products. The charges and fees are significantly higher than alternative investments offering the same choices. Mutual funds and ETFs can carry much lower expenses with the same type of underlying investments. Also see the above list of charges and fees.
- The benefit to the owner is usually not as great as the projected potential.
- Your principal is subject to large surrender charges (up to 7%, sometimes greater) if you need your money during the early years of the contract. The surrender charges decline over time, but that can be as long as 10 years.
- You may have to pay a 10% tax penalty if you withdraw money before 59½.
- Many features of the annuity may not be needed by the owner, but the charges for those features are in the contract.

- Tax deferral is available in IRAs and retirement accounts which can carry much lower expenses.
- They are marketed to seniors inappropriately with undisclosed risk in securities markets.
- Some insurance companies market contracts with a "bonus credit" feature but fail to disclose that the additional costs and expenses added to an annuity with this feature can eliminate any benefit from the bonus.

Variable annuities have long been high expense insurance products which are great income generators—for insurance companies and their sales force. But they have been poor investment choices for savers and investors looking for income from their savings.

With the stock market crash of 2008-2009, variable annuities become even more expensive for investors. Insurance companies "are raising prices and fees on some of their most popular investment products: variable annuities that promise market gains with no risk, and a lifetime stream of income. These moves suggest a problem that critics have long suspected: Many insurance companies radically underestimated the cost of hedging their guarantees in a market meltdown."[29]

Using Fixed Annuities

So, what about annuities? Is there a role for annuities in your retirement planning? Yes, there may be one proper use of an annuity in your retirement plan. A *fixed annuity* is appropriate for people who want to be assured of a steady stream of income which they will not outlive.

Forget the exotic features and bells and whistles promoted with some annuities. They are great income generators, but not for the annuity owner. Annuity salespeople love them. Their income stream is fattened and life is good.

Ask yourself the question I posed in Chapter 2, Rule 3 - Avoid the Big Mistakes: "Who benefits from this?" It had better be you. It's your money, your investment plan, and your retirement. Do not be enticed by the illusion of high reward with no risk.

If you must have a guaranteed income which you cannot outlive, consider an immediate fixed annuity. This annuity will take your lump sum contribution and immediately begin to provide you with periodic payments.

For singles, the best payout choice for income that you will not outlive is either…

- your lifetime for a specific minimum term (number of years) or
- lifetime with a lump sum to beneficiaries.

Either of these options will let you determine the minimum amount you will receive from the annuity and help you evaluate different annuity offerings.

For couples, the best payout option is *your lifetime and the life of another with a guaranteed minimum number of years*. This option will assure that neither of you will outlive the income, and your estate will receive any funds not distributed within the guaranteed period.

The bottom line on payout options should be obvious. The

more guarantees you want and the longer the guaranteed payout period, the smaller the monthly payment.

If you worry about outliving your investments, consider using an immediate fixed annuity or a fixed annuity with a longevity rider. The peace of mind may be worth the fees paid to the insurance company for administrating a lifetime source of income.

If that's you, here are some suggestions for incorporating a fixed annuity into your retirement plan:

1. Purchase a fixed annuity that will provide a payment up to the maximum amount *needed to cover only your fixed monthly expenses*.
2. Invest the balance of your financial assets using an asset allocation of equities, fixed income, and cash equivalents as described in Sections 3 and 4.

When purchasing a fixed annuity in a period when interest rates have come down significantly, consider creating a ladder of annuities. This ladder is created when you purchase fixed annuities over time. That is, you don't commit all your annuity money at one time, but purchase a fixed annuity every year or two, depending upon your time horizon. This ladder, or series, of annuities will help keep you from locking in a rate on the annuity portion of your assets at an interest rate bottom.

For planning purposes, a fixed annuity should be considered part of the fixed-income asset allocation of your investment portfolio. For example, a fixed annuity with a guaranteed 5% return for your lifetime should be viewed as equivalent to a bond fund with a 5% yield.

An annuity is a contract between you and an insurance company. While the assets of insurance contracts are separate from the assets of the company, it's still critical that you be aware of the financial strength of the insurance company issuing the annuity. This is especially important for annuities with performance guarantees. As the recent stock market crash revealed, some well-established insurance companies, which made minimum income or withdrawal guarantees, are being hard-pressed to meet those obligations. "After the market meltdown, the ratings agencies downgraded many insurers because the guarantees the insurers were offering were too generous, potentially sticking them with big payouts to annuity holders whose accounts lost a lot of money. As a result, many insurers pulled back on these guarantees and raised their fees..."[30]

Before purchasing an annuity, check the A.M. Best rating of the insurance company selling the annuity. A.M. Best is a credit rating organization that provides an independent opinion of insurance companies' financial strength. A.M. Best describes its rating as "an opinion of an insurer's ability to meet its obligations to policyholders... for an intermediate period, generally defined as the next 12 to 36 months." A guide to their ratings and methodologies may be viewed on their web site, www.ambest.com/ratings/guide.asp .

An abbreviated list of the A.M. Best Financial Strength Ratings:

A++, A+ (Superior).

A, A- (Excellent).

There are lower quality ratings from A.M. Best, but you should avoid any company with less than an A rating. This is not a linear scale. There is a vast difference between A++ and A-.

Also check the National Organization of Life & Health Insurance Guaranty Association's web site (www.nolhga.com/policyholderinfo/main.cfm/location/ga) for links to each state's guaranty association site. These state association web sites provide details about the amount of guaranteed coverage on a policy issued by insurance companies in the state, should they be unable to meet their obligations.

After thoughtful consideration, if you feel a fixed annuity is a good fit in your retirement plan, guard against the temptation to select a high fixed rate, guaranteed income, or withdrawal annuity from a less than financially sound company.

Summary of Annuity Characteristics

Immediate Annuity - payout period starts immediately at the time of purchase.

Deferred Annuity - payout period begins at a future date; offers appreciation potential during an accumulation period prior to commencement of the payout (annuitization).

Fixed Annuity - provides a fixed payout for lifetime(s) and/or specified period.

Variable Annuity - value of the annuity is based on performance of invested portfolio; payout may offer guaranteed income with excess appreciation dependent upon variable investments.

Chapter Questions

1. What are the two types of annuities?

2. Describe the purpose of the annuity's accumulation phase.

3. What characterizes the payout phase?

4. List several variable annuity concerns.

5. List several annuity payout options. Which options provide guarantees of minimum amounts of income payout?

6. Which payout option does not provide a guaranteed minimum payout amount?

7. What does a longevity rider in an annuity offer?

8. List several reasons why you might purchase a fixed annuity.

Chapter 21
Wrapping It Up

Chapter Objectives

- Realize we can't control events.
- Understand we can make choices.
- Understand our choices will have consequences.
- See the need to develop and stay with a plan.

So how are you feeling? I asked that question in the Introduction of this book after I had reviewed the events of the Financial Tsunami—events that affected our emotions and reactions to the tumultuous times of 2008 and 2009. After reading this book, are you able to see events such as economic cycles and stock market fluctuations any differently? Do you see the reality that some events are beyond your control and that how you respond to them is critical to staying on course, meeting your goals, and experiencing confidence in the midst of those events?

There are fundamental occurrences in our lives which we can't control or eliminate, such as aging, the arrival of retirement, and the cycles in the economy. But we can set goals and make plans to accommodate these events. We can choose how we will balance consumption with saving and investing. We can live in the present as we make plans for the future.

Retirement will be the harvest of what we plant during our working years. It will produce the enjoyment afforded us from balancing our consumption with saving and planning for retirement, or it will become the reality of our past consumption without regard for the future. The choice is ours.

In the Introduction, I set some goals for this book and for you. I hope that I have met those goals and that you will be able to set and meet your goals by understanding the benefits that are possible from implementing these fundamental principles:

- Taking responsibility for your own retirement planning and lifestyle choices is the critical first step. (Chapter 1)
- Understanding that your emotions, if left unchecked, can negatively impact your financial health. (Chapter 2)
- Your retirement goals should be established before you develop your investment plan. (Chapter 1)
- Preparing a cash flow analysis is essential to controlling your spending and savings. (Chapter 3)
- Preparing a budget—both before and after retirement—provides the discipline needed to achieve your goals. (Chapters 3 & 15)
- Balancing your "needs" and "wants" and controlling your spending are key factors in achieving your goals. (Chapter 1)
- Developing a realistic investment plan—one you can live with—is a critical step to achieving your goals. (Chapters 7, 8, 9)
- Implementing basic, time-tested investing and retirement planning principles is fundamental. (Chapters 7, 8, 9)
- Being consistent and staying with your plan will help you ride out financial turbulence. (Chapter 6)
- Periodically reviewing and rebalancing your investments to conform to your employment/retirement status and desired

asset allocation is important. (Chapter 14)

- Taking inappropriate risk in order to "make-up" for starting to save and invest late in life or to recover from past mistakes/losses, is a sure course to disaster. (Chapter 2)
- Transitioning into an active retirement can contribute to your mental and physical health.
- Educating yourself and staying informed about investment choices and retirement issues is just as important in retirement as it is during your working years.

You should now understand the relationship between your spending and investing habits during your working years and the impact this will have on your choices for a retirement lifestyle. You cannot save and invest what you don't have. Deferring some of your "wants" today, will have a positive impact on your ability to meet your income "needs" tomorrow.

You should also understand that setting an asset allocation that conforms to your tolerance for risk is critical to the long-term success of your investment plan. If you are not confident and comfortable with your allocation, you will be more likely to stray from or abandon your plan during times of economic and stock market turbulence.

Also remember that the protection afforded by asset diversification, by investing in index mutual funds and ETFs, offers investors the best, most cost effective route to investing success.

Whether you choose to be actively or passively involved in maintaining your portfolio, you need to stay informed regarding your investment choices and how they impact your retirement goals. If you choose to utilize the life-cycle/target-date funds, be careful to select a fund that matches your desired asset allocation; don't choose a fund based on its "date for retirement" alone. There can be significant differences between the asset allocation of funds with similar "dates." Don't assume that a fund with a date close to your retirement date will match your desired asset allocation. Be sure you check the fund's current asset allocation before making an investment decision.

When you retire, another critical decision will be how much to withdraw each year from your financial assets for living expenses. The withdrawal rate decision should take into account your…

- Age.
- Health.
- Retirement income needs.
- Desire to leave an inheritance.

One of your goals should be that your financial assets last as long as you do. The best Monte Carlo simulations can offer only a probability of achieving that goal, not a guarantee. Therefore, without knowing your specific situation, I recommend that when you begin retirement, you set an initial annual withdrawal rate of 4%. Depending upon personal factors, such as your age, adjust the initial withdrawal rate to fit your desires and comfort level. Obviously, the less you withdraw from your savings/investments, the greater the potential for additional growth and the longer those assets will last. If a financial tsunami like the one in 2008 occurs on the eve of your retirement, delaying retirement, deferring withdrawals, or significantly reducing the initial withdrawals can help to reduce the negative impact. Smaller or deferred withdrawals at the start of retirement can provide the greatest positive boost to the longevity of your financial assets.

I hope you also realize there is more to retirement than finances. The time we spend with family, friends, and chosen activities can make an impact on future generations that will remain long after we are gone and our material assets have passed on to others. The money we leave to others is a poor substitute for the time we can invest in people and the values we can share that will have eternal consequences.

I believe you will discover, as I have, that time is our most precious asset. It cannot be increased or recaptured if lost. Time can only be wasted or invested well.

All the goal setting, planning, and education that you can handle will do you no good if you don't develop and implement your *investing for retirement* plan. You "gotta" get serious.

Appendix A
Investing for Retirement Checklist

(PDF download available at www.InvestorTrainer.com/ebook/AppA.pdf)

√	Steps to Developing an Investing for Retirement Plan	Reference
	Prepare your list of retirement goals. What retirement lifestyle do you want and expect?	Chapter 1
	Prepare your Cash Flow analysis. What are you earning and spending?	Chapter 3, Appendix C - Cash flow Worksheet
	Prepare your personal Balance Sheet. Determine what you own, what you owe, and your Net Worth?	Chapter 4, Appendix C - Balance Sheet Net Worth Worksheet
	How many years until you retire? If you are unsure, use a best case estimate.	
	Set specific savings & investment goals that will accommodate your retirement goals.	Chapter 3, Chapter 15
	Review your goals (years until retirement, lifestyle and financial) for reasonableness. Adjust goals as necessary.	
	Determine your investing temperament and risk tolerance.	Chapter 2 Rule 1, Chapter 6

	Determine your asset allocation that matches your risk tolerance, years until retirement, and goals.	Chapter 7
	Select investments for each asset class of your asset allocation.	Chapter 9, Chapter 10
	Review your investments and allocations in relation to historical returns to determine probability of attaining long-term goals.	Chapter 7, Chapter 8
	Make any necessary adjustments to your investment plan in response to the review of probability.	
	Contact a brokerage firm, mutual fund company, or bank and open appropriate investment accounts (taxable brokerage account and IRA).	Chapter 11
	Make initial deposit into the investment account(s).	Chapter 11
	Call broker or mutual fund company and place orders for your selected mutual funds or ETFs.	Chapter 11
	Review trade confirmation (mail or online) for accuracy of the purchase.	
	Periodically review brokerage statements for account activity and trades.	Chapter 12
	Annually rebalance asset classes to match desired asset allocation.	Chapter 14

	At least annually prepare a cash flow analysis to see if income and expenses are on track and determine if additional deposits are possible for the long-term investment accounts.	Chapter 3
	Once your retirement date is set, implement the Retirement Checklist in Chapter 15 for pre-retirement activities.	Chapter 15
	Review your most recent Social Security and employer sponsored retirement plan estimates.	Chapter 14
	Prepare a Retirement Budget. Estimate how much you will need for the lifestyle you desire. Determine amounts and sources of income.	Chapter 3, Chapter 5, Chapter 15
	Determine your withdrawal options. Review your portfolio and retirement budget.	Chapter 18, Chapter 19
	Prepare to transition into retirement. Use the Retirement Worksheet and Checklist.	Chapter 15, Appendix F
	Continue to manage and rebalance your portfolio.	Chapter 18

Appendix B
Risk Tolerance and Investing Experience Evaluation Worksheet

(PDF download available at www.InvestorTrainer.com/ebook/AppB.pdf)

This worksheet provides a self-evaluation of your risk tolerance and investing experience. This evaluation will help you see…

- Your risk tolerance level - how much risk are you comfortable taking.
- Your emotional reactions to investment fluctuations - how you will respond to market fluctuations.
- Your investing experience.

Using the questions which begin on the next page, take the **Risk Tolerance evaluation**:

1. Review each question and circle the response which best describes your emotion or purpose.
2. Total the count for the responses in each column - Conservative, Moderate, or Aggressive. Each circled response has a value of one. The column with the greatest total count indicates your orientation toward a risk tolerance. If you chose responses 1A and 4A, you may not be an investor.

In the **Recognize Investing Experience** section -

1. Select your answers for the four questions.
2. Use the scoring key to assign a value to your answers for each question.
3. Calculate your score by totaling the Your Values column to help see your Investing Experience.

			Risk Tolerance		
			CONSERVATIVE	MODERATE	AGGRESSIVE
1.	How do you feel when your financial investments (stocks, mutual funds) are worth less than you paid for the investment six months prior?				
	A.	I was really foolish to have bought in the first place. (Not an investor.)			
	B.	If the fundamental outlook for the company is still positive, this may be an opportunity to purchase additional shares.		X	X
	C.	I need to wait and see if the price recovers before making additional purchases.	X		
2.	How do you feel when you see/read stories in the news media about a recession or downturn in the economy?				
	A.	Fearful for my investments.	X		
	B.	A possible future opportunity to invest in stocks/funds, but not right now.	X	X	

C.	Neither fearful nor opportunistic, I remain committed to my investment plan.			X

3.	If you have $10,000 invested in a stock or mutual fund, and after 6 months the value dropped 20%, what would you do?			
A.	Sell & move to another investment.	X		
B.	Add to the investment.		X	X
C.	Make no changes.		X	

4.	When I invest in the financial markets, my primary goal is...			
A.	Safety of principal. I do not want to lose money. (Not an investor.)			
B.	To generate immediate spendable income from the investment.	X		
C.	To provide growth of the investments with modest current income.	X		
D.	To provide better than average long-term growth; income is not a goal.		X	
E.	Assume greater degree of risk for maximum potential growth.			X

5.	Which of the following scenarios best describes the average annual return you would be willing to accept after considering the best and worst annual returns your choice might generate for a given year? For example, if you are unwilling to experience more than a negative 6% return in any year, then scenario B, with the average annual return of 7%, is the best choice.					
	Acceptable Average	Best Year	Worst Year			
A.	4%	5%	3%	X		
B.	7%	15%	-6%	X		
C.	9%	25%	-12%		X	
D.	11%	35%	-25%			X
E.	13%	50%	-40%			X
Your TOTAL count for each column:						

Which column had the largest number of responses - Conservative, Moderate or Aggressive?

Recognize Investing Experience:

_____ 1. My understanding of financial markets is…

A. A complete mystery.

B. Limited, but I think it is a good place to invest for the long-term.

C. Good knowledge of long-term growth and income opportunities.

_____ 2. I have been an investor in stocks/bonds/mutual funds for…

A. Never have invested.
B. Less than 5 years.
C. 5 to 10 years.
D. 10 years or longer.

_____ 3. The **stock market** is best suited for achieving which investment goal(s)?

A. Maximize earnings on short-term savings.
B. Long term growth.
C. Some growth, but primarily income.
D. Generating monthly income.

_____ 4. I feel confident in my ability to select the following investments: (Choose all that you have knowledge of.)

A. Certificate of Deposit or money market.
B. Equity mutual fund.
C. Individual stock purchase.
D. Individual bond purchase.
E. Bond mutual fund.
F. New stock issues - IPOs.

The scoring key is on the next page.

Scoring key for Investing Experience - numeric value for each possible answer:

Question	A	B	C	D	E	F	Your Value
1.	0	1	2				
2.	0	1	2	3			
3.	0	2	0	0			
4.	0	1	2	2	1	3	
						Your score	

Investing Experience	Score
None	0 - 3
Beginner	4 - 7
Somewhat	8 - 12
Experienced	13+

Appendix C
Financial Worksheets

(PDF download available at www.InvestorTrainer.com/ebook/AppC.pdf)

CASH FLOW WORKSHEET

INCOME	MONTHLY AMOUNT
Your salary/wages	
Total Deductions:	
Taxes, Social Security, Medicare	
Other deductions	
Your Net Take-Home	
Spouse Salary/Wages	
Total Deductions:	
Taxes, Social Security, Medicare	
Other Deductions	
Spouse's Net Take-Home	
Total Net Salary/Wages (add Net Take-Home amounts)	
Interest Earned	
Investments - Dividends	
Social Security Received	
Retirement Income Received	
Miscellaneous	

Other income:	
Total Monthly Gross Disposable Income **(Line A)**	

EXPENSES-NONDISCRETIONARY	**MONTHLY AMOUNT**
Mortgage/Rent	
Home/Renter Insurance	
Home Repairs & Maintenance	
Property Taxes, Fees	
Other Housing Expenses	
Transportation: Vehicle Payments	
Gas & Oil	
Maintenance & Repairs	
Insurance	
Commuting	
Groceries	
Clothing	
Personal Care Products	
Child Care, Babysitters	
Medical: Doctors, Dentists, Other	
Prescriptions	
Supplies	
Medical Insurance Premiums[1]	
Utilities: Electricity, Gas, Oil	

[1] Not included in income deductions

Water, Sewer, Fees	
Telephone	
Credit Card Interest, Fees	
Other Loan Interest, Fees	
Other Taxes, Tax Payments	
Dining Out	
Clothing accessories	
Travel	
Entertainment	
Household Furnishings, Misc Items	
Pet Expenses	
Subscriptions & Dues	
Gifts	
Miscellaneous	
Total Monthly Expenses **(Line B)**	

ADDITIONS TO SAVINGS & INVESTMENTS	**MONTHLY AMOUNT**
401(k)s, 403(b)s, Other Plans[2]	
Traditional IRAs	
Roth IRAs	
Investment Accounts/Mutual Funds	
Other: (CDs, Money Market, Savings Accounts)	
Total Additions to Savings & Investments **(Line C)**	

[2] If not deducted from Net Take-Home on Income Analysis.

NET DISCRETIONARY INCOME CALCULATION

Line 1. TOTAL MONTHLY GROSS DISPOSABLE INCOME	*From:* Line A	
Line 2. TOTAL EXPENSES	Line B	
Line 3. **NET DISCRETIONARY INCOME**	Subtract Line 2 from Line 1	
Line 4. TOTAL ADDITION TO SAVINGS & INVESTMENTS	Line C	
Line 5. NET MONTHLY SURPLUS OR SHORTAGE	Subtract Line 4 from Line 3	

BALANCE SHEET - NET WORTH WORKSHEET

ASSETS	AMOUNT
Cash	
Savings (CDs, money market, savings accts)	
Market value of residence	
Other real estate	
Investments:	
Stocks, ETFs, mutual funds, etc.	
Bonds, ETFs, bond funds	
Other investments	
Retirement accounts:	
401(k)s	
IRAs	
Vested pensions	
Personal property (household items, artwork, etc)	
Vehicles	
Other:	
TOTAL ASSETS **(Line TA)**	

BALANCE SHEET - NET WORTH WORKSHEET

LIABILITIES	AMOUNT
Home Loan	
Other Real Estate Loans	
Vehicle Loans	
Personal Bank Loans	
Credit Card Debts	
Borrowed From Retirement Plans	
Investment Debt (Margin Loans)	
Other Debts	
TOTAL LIABILITIES **(Line TL)**	

NET WORTH CALCULATION From:

Line 1. TOTAL ASSETS	Line TA	
Line 2. TOTAL LIABILITIES	Line TL	
Line 3. **NET WORTH**	Subtract line 2 from line 1	

EXAMPLES
Abbreviated Financial Worksheets

EXAMPLE: CASH FLOW WORKSHEET

INCOME	**MONTHLY AMOUNT**
Your salary/wages	6,000
Deductions:	
Taxes, Social Security, Medicare	1,500
Other deductions	420
Your Net Take-Home	4,080
Spouse's Net Take-Home	2,250
Total Net Salary/Wages (add Net Take-Home amts.)	6,330
Interest	50
Investments - Dividends	48
Social Security Received	
Miscellaneous	
Other:	
Total Monthly Gross Disposable Income (Line A)	6,428

EXAMPLE: CASH FLOW WORKSHEET - CONT.

EXPENSES	**MONTHLY AMOUNT**
Mortgage/Rent	1,300
Home/Renter Insurance	80
Home Repairs & Maintenance	400
Property Taxes, Fees	100
Other Housing Expenses	275
Transportation: Vehicle Payments	190
Gas & Oil	130
Maintenance & Repairs	100
Insurance	400
Commuting	
Groceries	520
Dining Out	200
Travel	200
Entertainment	120
Subscriptions & dues	120
Gifts	150
Miscellaneous	350
TOTAL EXPENSES (Line B)	5,035

EXAMPLE: CASH FLOW WORKSHEET - CONT.

ADDITIONS TO SAVINGS & INVESTMENTS	MONTHLY AMOUNT
401(k)s, 403(b)s, Other Plans[3]	
Traditional IRAs	
Roth IRAs	916
Investment Accounts/Mutual Funds	100
Other: (CDs, Money Market, Savings Accounts)	
College savings acct	150
Total Additions to Savings & Investments (Line C)	1,166

[3] If not deducted from Net Take-Home on Income Analysis.

EXAMPLE: NET DISCRETIONARY INCOME CALCULATION

	From:	
Line 1. TOTAL MONTHLY GROSS DISPOSABLE INCOME	Line A	6,428
Line 2. TOTAL EXPENSES	Line B	5,035
Line 3. **NET DISCRETIONARY INCOME**	Subtract Line 2 from Line 1	1,393
Line 4. TOTAL ADDITION TO SAVINGS & INVESTMENTS	Line C	1,166
Line 5. NET MONTHLY SURPLUS OR SHORTAGE	Subtract Line 4 from Line 3	227

EXAMPLE: BALANCE SHEET - NET WORTH WORKSHEET

ASSETS	**AMOUNT**
Cash	2,600
Savings (CDs, money market, savings accts)	7,500
Market value of residence	200,000
Other real estate	
Investments:	
Stocks, ETFs, mutual funds, etc.	18,000
Bonds, ETFs, bond funds	5,000
Retirement accounts:	
401(k)s	230,000
IRAs	100,000
Vested pensions	
Personal property (household items, artwork, etc)	30,000
Vehicles	48,000
Other:	
TOTAL ASSETS **(Line TA)**	641,100

EXAMPLE:
BALANCE SHEET - NET WORTH WORKSHEET - CONT.

LIABILITIES	AMOUNT
Home Loan	145,000
Other Real Estate Loans	
Vehicle Loans	32,000
Personal Bank Loans	
Credit Card Debts	4,200
Borrowed From Retirement Plans	
Investment Debt (Margin Loans)	
Other Debts	
TOTAL LIABILITIES **(Line TL)**	181,200

NET WORTH CALCULATION From:

Line 1. TOTAL ASSETS	Line TA	641,000
Line 2. TOTAL LIABILITIES	Line TL	181,200
Line 3. **NET WORTH**	Subtract line 2 from line 1	459,800

RETIREMENT BUDGET WORKSHEET

INCOME	**YOU**	**SPOUSE**
Social Security		
Employer Retirement Plans (401(k), 403(b), etc.)		
Employer Pensions		
IRA Withdrawals		
Interest		
Dividends from Investments		
Withdrawals from Investment Accounts		
Rents, Royalties		
Annuity		
Part or Full-Time Employment (Net Pay)		
Other Steady Source of Income		
Total Monthly Income		

RETIREMENT BUDGET WORKSHEET - CONT.

EXPENSES	**MONTHLY AMOUNT**
Mortgage/Rent	
Home/Renter Insurance	
Home Repairs & Maintenance	
Property Taxes, Fees	
Other Housing Expenses	
Transportation:	
Vehicle Payments	
Gas & Oil	
Maintenance & Repairs	
Insurance	
Commuting	
Groceries	
Dining Out	
Personal Care Products	
Child Care, Babysitters	
Medical:	
Doctors, Dentists, Other	
Prescriptions	
Supplies	

Medical Insurance Premiums[4]	
Utilities:	
Electricity, Gas, Oil	
Water, Sewer, Fees	
Telephone	
TV/High Speed Internet	
Credit Card Debt Payment	
Other Loan Payments	
Clothing	
Other Taxes, Tax Payments	
Pet Expenses	
Household Furnishings, Misc Items	
Travel	
Entertainment	
Subscriptions & Dues	
Gifts	
Miscellaneous	
Total Expenses	

[4] Not included in Income or Social Security deductions

Total Monthly Income	
Total Monthly Expenses	
Estimated Monthly Cash Flow (Income - Expenses)	

(This page left blank.)

Appendix D
Asset Allocation Worksheets

(PDF download available at www.InvestorTrainer.com/ebook/AppD.pdf)

Your risk tolerance (see Chapter 6):____________

Your number of years until retirement: _________

For a clearer understanding of the information presented in the Appendix D worksheets, you download and print this appendix.

Instructions for using Table D-1:

1. On the top row, circle the number of years until you retire.
2. On the second row, under the number of years until retirement column which you circled in step 1, select and circle the column letter (Conservative, Moderate, or Aggressive) which reflects your risk tolerance.
3. Read down the selected column (C, M, or A) for the appropriate percentages of each asset class.

Table D-1 reveals the changing asset allocation percentages for each class of assets as you move closer to retirement. See Chapter 7 for additional discussion of asset allocations.

Table D-1:
Asset Allocation Percentages by Asset Class

Years Until Retirement	15+			8 – 14		
Risk Tolerance: **C**onservative **M**oderate **A**ggressive	**C**	**M**	**A**	**C**	**M**	**A**
Equities	60	75	100	50	70	90
Fixed Income	40	25	0	45	30	10
Cash Equivalents	0	0	0	5	0	0
Years Until Retirement	4 - 7			1 - 3		
Risk Tolerance: **C**onservative **M**oderate **A**ggressive	**C**	**M**	**A**	**C**	**M**	**A**
Equities	45	55	75	40	50	65
Fixed Income	50	40	25	55	45	30
Cash Equivalents	5	5	0	5	5	5

Table D-1, continued.

Years Until Retirement	0 Retirement		
Risk Tolerance: **C**onservative **M**oderate **A**ggressive	**C**	**M**	**A**
Equities	30	40	60
Fixed Income	60	55	35
Cash Equivalents	10	5	5

Table D-2: Asset Class – Equities Allocation

Table D-2 presents the allocation percentage for each of the 3 equity groups. For example, an investor with a moderate risk tolerance who is 10 years from retirement should divide the equity allocation into 25% large capitalization equities, 20% small and medium capitalization equities, and 25% foreign equities. See Chapter 7 for more discussion on asset allocation.

Years Until Retirement	15+			8 - 14		
Risk Tolerance: **C**onservative **M**oderate **A**ggressive	**C**	**M**	**A**	**C**	**M**	**A**
Equity Groups:						
Large Capitalization	20	20	25	20	25	20
Small / Medium Cap	20	30	50	15	20	45
Foreign	20	25	25	15	25	25
Total Equity Allocation	**60**	**75**	**100**	**50**	**70**	**90**

Table D-2, continued.

Years Until Retirement	4 – 7			1 - 3		
Risk Tolerance: **C**onservative **M**oderate **A**ggressive	**C**	**M**	**A**	**C**	**M**	**A**
Equity Groups:						
Large Capitalization	15	15	20	15	15	15
Small / Medium Cap	15	20	35	10	20	30
Foreign	15	20	20	15	15	20
Total Equity Allocation	**45**	**55**	**75**	**40**	**50**	**65**

Years Until Retirement	0 Retirement		
Risk Tolerance: **C**onservative **M**oderate **A**ggressive	**C**	**M**	**A**
Equity Groups:			
Large Capitalization	15	15	15
Small / Medium Cap	5	10	25
Foreign	10	15	20
Total Equity Allocation	**30**	**40**	**60**

Table D-3: Asset Class: Fixed Income Allocation

Table D-3 shows the allocation percentage of the fixed-income class in two categories – US Government securities and Corporate bonds. The bottom row shows the total of the two categories for the fixed-income allocation (from Table D-1).

Years Until Retirement	15+			8 - 14		
Risk Tolerance: **C**onservative **M**oderate **A**ggressive	**C**	**M**	**A**	**C**	**M**	**A**
US Government Inflation-Protected Bonds TIPS	20	15	0	25	20	0
Corporates: Total Bond Mkt (all sectors)	20	10	0	20	10	10
Total Fixed-Income Allocation	**40**	**25**	**0**	**45**	**30**	**10**

Table D-3, continued.

Years Until Retirement	4 – 7			1 - 3		
Risk Tolerance: **C**onservative **M**oderate **A**ggressive	**C**	**M**	**A**	**C**	**M**	**A**
US Government Inflation-Protected Bonds TIPS	30	20	10	35	30	10
Corporates: Total Bond Mkt (all sectors)	20	20	15	20	15	20
Total Fixed-Income Allocation	**50**	**40**	**25**	**55**	**45**	**30**

Table D-3, continued.

Years Until Retirement	0 Retirement		
Risk Tolerance: **C**onservative **M**oderate **A**ggressive	**C**	**M**	**A**
US Government Inflation-Protected Bonds TIPS	40	35	15
Corporates: Total Bond Mkt (all sectors)	20	20	20
Total Fixed-Income Allocation	**60**	**55**	**35**

Table D-4: Personal Asset Allocation & Investment Category

Select your investments for each of the following asset class and sub-classes –

- Equity –
  - Large Cap
  - Small/Mid Cap
  - Foreign
- Fixed-income –
  - US Government Bonds
  - Corporate Bonds
- Cash Equivalents

Make a list of your selected investments with columns headings for the following items–

- Name of the investment.
- Symbol of the investment (fund/ETF symbol).
- Amount invested.
- Percentage of total portfolio.

A full-size worksheet is available for downloading and printing at www. InvestorTrainer.com/ebook/AppD.pdf.

Table D-5A: Worksheet for Rebalancing Your Portfolio

Make a list of all the investments in your portfolio, including any in a defined-contribution account for which you have management responsibility.

For each investment, include the current dollar value and percent of total portfolio – grouping and totaling each investment in one of the asset classes and sub-categories.

Compare the allocation percentage for each class to your desired asset allocation. Rebalance your assets once a year by buying and selling securities as necessary to achieve your desired asset allocation.

A full-size worksheet is available for downloading and printing at www.InvestorTrainer.com/ebook/AppD.pdf.

Review Table D-5B: Example and Instructions for using Worksheet for Rebalancing Your Portfolio (in the download PDF) for a completed example of using Table D-5A, before you begin.

Instructions for using the Table D5-A PDF download version -

1. Using the latest investment/fund statements, list all of your investments with their names and current dollar value in the first 2 columns.
2. Using the latest fund annual report or fund research web site, distribute the percentages across in the four asset class columns (large cap, small/mid cap, foreign, and fixed income) for each fund.
3. Calculate a dollar value for each asset class for each fund (current fund value x asset class percentage = asset class value).
   Example: 50,000 x 75% = 37,500.
4. Total the dollar value columns, and put the totals for each column on the line "Current Portfolio Totals."
5. Using your asset allocations from Chapter 7, fill in, on the "Your Asset Allocation % Goal" line, the percentages for your asset allocation goal in each of the four asset class columns.

6. Calculate your asset allocation dollar goal (Current Portfolio Total x Your Asset Allocation % Goal) for each of the four asset class columns. Example: 170,000 x 25% = 42,500.
7. For each of the four asset class columns, subtract Your Asset Allocation $ Goal from the Current Portfolio Totals. The result is the dollar amount which must be bought or sold to rebalance each asset class, and maintain your desired asset allocation.
Example: 37,500 – 42,500 = -5,000; you should purchase $5,000 of securities for this asset class.

Appendix E
Asset Class Investment Choices

(A formatted PDF download is available at www.InvestorTrainer.com /ebook/AppE.pdf)

Each security listed includes: Fund name, fund type (MF = mutual fund or ETF = exchange-traded fund), symbol, and expense ratio percentage.

Table: E-1 Equity Large Cap Category –
Large Capitalization:
- Vanguard 500 Index, MF, VFINX, .18%
- Schwab S&P 500 Index Fund, MF, SWPPX, .09%
- Vanguard Large Cap Index, ETF, VV, .12%
- iShares:Morningstar Large Cap, ETF, JKD, .20%
- Vanguard Total Stock Mkt. ETF, ETF, VTI, .07%
- Fidelity Spartan Total Mkt. Index, MF, FSTMX, .10%

Table: E-2 Equity Mid/Small Cap Category -
Mid Capitalization:
- iShares S&P Mid Cap 400 Value Index, ETF, IJJ, .25%
- Vanguard Mid Cap Value Index, ETF, VOE, .14%

Small Capitalization:
- Vanguard Small Cap Index, ETF, VB, .14%
- iShares S&P 600 Small Cap Value, ETF, IJS, .25%

Table: E-3 Equity Foreign/International Category -
- Vanguard Total International Stock Index, MF, VGTSX, .27%
- Vanguard FTSE All World Except US Index, ETF, VEU, .25%
- iShares MSCI Emerging Markets Index, ETF, EEM, .72%

Table: E-4 Fixed Income Category -

US Government issues:

Vanguard Inflation-Protected Securities, MF, VIPSX, .25%

iShares Barclays TIPS Bond (Treasury Inflation-Protected Securities), ETF, TIP, .20%

iShares Barclays 3-7 Year Treasury Bond Index, ETF, IEI, .15%

Vanguard Short-Term Treasury Fund, MF, VFISX, .22%

Corporates:

Vanguard Total Bond Market Index, MF, VBMFX, .22%

Vanguard Intermediate-Term Bond Index, MF, VBIIX, .22%

Appendix F
Setting Goals & Retirement Date Worksheet

(PDF download available at www.InvestorTrainer.com/ebook/AppF.pdf)

1. Review your retirement goals. List your goals for these categories:

   Employment:

   Financial:

   - Debt elimination/reduction:
   - Savings & spending:

   Personal:

   - Family/Friends:
   - Ministry:
   - Travel:
   - Recreation/Hobbies:
   - Other activities:

   Residence:

   - Current residence: satisfied, sell, fix up ________
   - Move to: house, apartment, retirement community, less expensive community, other: ________________

   Other goals: ____________________________________
2. Prioritize your goals.
3. Review or prepare your current Cash Flow Analysis.
4. Prepare a Retirement Budget.

   Calculate the total current value of your investment portfolio –

   - Employer defined-contribution plans _____________
   - IRAs _____________
   - Other retirement plan assets _____________
   - Brokerage accounts _____________
   - Mutual fund accounts _____________
   - Bank, savings balances _____________
   - Other financial assets _____________

   Total Portfolio/Financial Assets: _____________

5. What rate of withdrawal will you take from your portfolio each year? __________%
   Amount of annual withdrawal =_______________
   (Withdrawal rate x Total Portfolio)
   Amount of Monthly Withdrawal_______________(A)

6. Calculate your monthly retirement income from fixed sources:
   Social Security _________________
   Employer defined-benefit _________________
   Annuity income _________________
   Other _________________
   Total monthly income from fixed sources: _________________(B)
7. Calculate your estimated total monthly retirement income:
   Monthly withdrawal from portfolio: _________________(A)
   Total monthly income from fixed sources: _________________(B)
   Estimated Total Monthly Retirement Income: _________________(A+B)

8. Determine when you can retire:
   Will you have any debt when you start retirement?
   How much is your debt payment(s) each month?
   If you have debt, can you pay it off before retirement starts?
   Will your retirement income cover your estimated living expenses?
   If your expenses exceed your retirement income, what will you do to accommodate this?
   Work full or part-time?
   Reduce anticipated expenses: make a list of items which could be reduced.
   Recalculate your retirement budget.
   What is the earliest date you *could* retire from your current job?

What is the date you *would like* to retire from your current job?

Based on your estimated Retirement Budget, income forecast, and debt payoff schedule, on what date do you think you *could afford* to retire?

Glossary

12b-1 fee – a marketing or distribution fee charged by some mutual fund companies against the fund's assets. Generally this fee is out of favor today but may still be found in high-expense loaded funds.

401(k) – an employer sponsored retirement plan into which the employer and the employee make pre-tax contributions. The employer usually makes a minimal contribution plus a matching contribution up to a certain percentage, as an inducement for employee participation. These are known as defined-contribution plans. The payout is based upon the value of the assets in the plan at retirement. See Defined-contribution plan.

Annuity - an insurance contract designed to provide a guaranteed income stream for the life of the annuity owner, the owner and another person's life, or for a fixed number of years. Annuities may be characterized as either immediate or deferred with regard to the commencement of the payout phase, and the payout amount may be either fixed or variable. These insurance contracts are best used in retirement planning to provide a fixed income for life. See Chapter 20 – What about Annuities? for more specifics and a discussion of the appropriate uses and potential abuses of annuities.

Asset - something you own; e.g., a house, personal property, stocks, mutual funds, cash, or a vehicle.

Asset Allocation – the distribution of a financial portfolio into the asset classes: equities (stocks), fixed income (bonds) and cash equivalents. See Chapter 7, Establishing Your Asset Allocation.

Asset Classes – categories of investments which offer different levels of risk and potential for return. The 3 major financial asset classes are: equities (stocks), for growth; fixed income (bonds), for steady income; and cash equivalents (money markets, CDs), which provide stability of principal but low return. See Chapter 7, Establishing Your Asset Allocation.

Balance sheet - a list of all your assets and liabilities (debts). The mathematical difference between your assets and liabilities is your net worth. This is a snapshot of your current financial situation. Seeing where you are financially is helpful in developing financial goals and investment plans for retirement. See Appendix C for worksheets to help you create your personal balance sheet.

Balanced Fund – a mutual fund which invests in all three asset classes in order to provide growth with income and preservation of principal. For example, a fund's assets may be distributed in equities (60%), fixed income (37%) and cash equivalents (3%). Check the fund prospectus before investing - there is no standard for balanced fund allocations.

Bear Market - refers to a declining market; usually used in reference to the stock market. The bears are going into hibernation and not buying stocks. In any market, when there are more sellers than buyers, the buyers gain the advantage and it becomes a buyer's market as prices tend to decline.

Bond – a financial instrument issued by a corporation or government authority which represents a debt of the issuer to the holder of the bond. Bonds pay a fixed rate of interest for a specific length of time. The interest is usually paid every six months, but this can vary depending upon the terms of the bond. At maturity, the original face value of the bond is paid to the current holder of the bond. Bonds are used in investor portfolios to provide steady income and relative price stability as compared to stocks.

Bond Ladder - a series of bonds with the maturities equally spread out over time. Usually an equal portion of the bonds matures each year. For example, in a 5-year bond ladder, one fifth of the portfolio would mature every year. Each year as 20 percent of the bond portfolio matures it is reinvested in new bonds with a 5-year maturity at the current interest rate. The bond ladder can help generate a higher average yield on the total bond portfolio. This technique also works well with CDs; see CD Ladder.

Bond rating - a quality rating on the ability of the issuer to repay the bond when it matures. Credit rating firms include Standard & Poor's Corporation, Moody's, and Fitch Ratings.

The ratings range:

AAA (highest quality investment grade)

AA (investment grade)

A (investment grade)

BBB (lowest investment grade)

BB thru C (non-investment grade; also called Junk bonds)

D (the bond is in default).

Bull Market - refers to an advancing (upward trending) market in which share prices are rising; usually used in reference to the stock market. The bulls are running. In any market, when there are more buyers than sellers, the sellers gain the advantage, and it becomes a seller's market where prices will tend to rise.

Capitulation - an event signaling that the stock market has reached a Bear Market bottom; when investors give up on stocks and the stock market and sell out; a period of extremely high volume of stock trades, when nothing but negative predictions and outlook for stocks and the economy is in the news; accompanied by major declines in the price of stocks. This is an emotional period for all investors, both seasoned and newcomers. Historically, this has offered the best opportunity for long-term investors—who fully understand market emotions and psychology—to make long-term investments. A thorough understanding of Rule 1 (see Chapter 1) is essential to handling this event in order to keep from making emotion-driven mistakes.

Cash equivalents – an asset class distinguished by stability of principal. The class includes cash, money market accounts, Certificates of Deposit, and short-term Treasury bills and commercial paper.

Cash flow - determining where the money comes from and where it is spent. An analysis of all of your sources of income and spending will reveal what you have left over to save or invest, or why you are increasing your debt obligations. This is a critical analysis in developing a budget, paying off debts, and developing a plan to invest for retirement. See Appendix C for worksheets to help with a cash flow analysis.

CD Ladder - a series of certificates of deposit, with maturities spread out evenly to a future date. As one CD matures, it is renewed for the maximum term of the ladder. For example, a 4-year CD ladder will contain CDs of 1-, 2-, 3-, and 4-year maturities, with 25% of the CDs maturing every year. This can help increase the yield over time and eliminate the chance of locking in a low interest rate at the bottom of an interest rate cycle on the full CD portfolio. See the example on the next page. Also, see Bond Ladder.

CDs in Ladder Maturities	% of CD Portfolio
12-Month CD	25
24-Month CD	25
36-Month CD	25
48-Month CD	25

Defined-benefit retirement plan - an employer-funded retirement plan which provides a *specific monthly benefit* during retirement. The benefit may be based upon a formula that includes the number of years of employment and salary level, or a specific dollar amount. These plans are disappearing today and are being replaced by defined-contribution plans. See defined-contribution retirement plan.

Defined-contribution retirement plan - an employer-sponsored retirement plan funded by the employer and employee. The plan establishes a formula or limit for employee and employer contributions. The payout at retirement, unknown during the accumulation phase, is determined by the accumulated value of the employee's account at retirement when withdrawals begin. The employee contributions and earnings are not taxed until withdrawn. Examples of such plans are 401(k), 403(b), 457, and SEP IRAs. See defined-benefit plan.

Discretionary income - the amount of income available after taxes and spending on basic needs (food, clothing, and shelter). After spending on the necessities and taxes, the remainder of income is spent as an individual chooses; it is discretionary. See Net Discretionary Income.

Disposable income - remainder of income after taxes. Gross income minus taxes leaves the amount of income available for spending, savings, and investment. See Gross Disposable Income.

Diversified, diversification - to be distributed among many different securities and industries. In financial terms - a diversified portfolio of stocks or bonds. Diversification provides the investor with safety by having assets distributed among many different securities, thus not having all your eggs (investments) in one basket (one stock). If one or a few stocks decline, other stocks in the portfolio may provide balance and offset. Diversification means owning multiple companies within multiple industries. This is one of the primary advantages of diversified mutual funds and ETFs.

Dollar Cost Averaging - investing a set amount of money into a fund at regular intervals; e.g., investing $100 a month into a mutual fund. The investment is made regardless of the market cycle or share price. This disciplined approach takes advantage of purchasing more shares in down markets, fewer shares in up markets, and removes our emotions from the investing decision.

Employee Stock Ownership Plan (ESOP) - a company-sponsored defined retirement plan in which the assets of the plan are in the stock of the company.

Exchange-traded fund (ETF) - a basket of stocks or bonds, similar in composition to a mutual fund. A share certificate, which represents ownership of a portion of the total portfolio of securities, is bought or sold on an exchange like a share of stock. Usually the ETF, such as the Vanguard Total Stock Market ETF, represents an index designed to track a particular group of stocks, or a bond index. Recently some ETFs have been introduced that are actively managed pools of stocks or bonds. Because the ETF shares trade on an exchange, they are usually less expensive to purchase or sell, and the trade can be transacted quickly, almost instantaneously. The per-share price of the ETF, like a stock, is set by the marketplace. Large institutional investors help keep the market price close to the true underlying value of the basket of stocks or bonds by being willing to buy or sell ETF shares when the market price moves away from the true value. In volatile markets, bond ETFs can have trouble tracking an index, due to the occasional limited availability of the bonds which are in the index. See Mutual Fund.

FDIC (Federal Deposit Insurance Corporation) – a United States government agency whose mission is "to maintain stability and public confidence in the nation's financial system by: insuring deposits, examining and supervising financial institutions…

and managing receiverships [failed banks].” The current insured amount is $250,000 per individual, per institution.

FICO Score - a credit score used to grade an individual’s credit risk. FICO was developed by Fair Isaac Corporation. It takes into account factors such as payment history, types of credit used, and amount of indebtedness. The FICO Score ranges from 350 to 850, with a score above 660 considered good. In 2008 a new score, dubbed FICO 08, was introduced which, it is hoped, will more accurately predict possible borrower default.

Flash Crash – the stock market plunge on May 6, 2010 which lasted less than an hour before prices returned to near where they were before the “plunge”. It is believed to have been caused by programmed trading, with a large sell order for S&P futures contracts.

Fundamental indexing - a fairly recent approach to building an index of equity securities based on fundamental values such as revenue, earnings, book value, dividends, or cash flow, as opposed to the more traditional indices based on market capitalization.

Fund of funds - a fund which invests in other mutual funds or uses other managers to make investments for the fund. These are usually sold as Limited Partnerships. This type of fund may allow the investor into sophisticated investment strategies, but at higher expense ratios.

Gross Disposable Income - a term used in this book to represent disposable income plus gross income from other sources, such as interest and dividends. This is typically the net inflow of cash to investors each month. It is your gross income from all sources after taxes are deducted on the wages portion only. This figure is useful in cash flow analysis.

Hedge fund - an unregistered investment fund which pools investors' money to make equity, fixed-income, or commodity investments. Hedge funds may use leverage (debt) and other sophisticated investment strategies to minimize (hedge) market risk or maximize gains from the price changes of their investments. These funds are limited to wealthy and financially sophisticated individuals. Hedge funds are not appropriate for most investors who are saving/investing for, or living in, retirement.

I-Bonds - United States Savings Bonds with a variable interest rate designed to reflect the rate of inflation based on the Consumer Price Index.

- Interest rate has 2 components - fixed for life of bond and variable to reflect CPI.
- Variable portion of the rate adjusts every 6 months.
- Interest earned is tax-deferred until cashed in.
- Interest compounds semiannually for up to 30 years.
- May be redeemed after 12 months.
- 3-month interest penalty if redeemed during first 5 years.
- In deflationary periods the rate never goes below zero and the accumulated principal does not decline.

As of January 1, 2008, there is a calendar year limit per individual (social security number) of $5000 for bonds issued in paper form and an additional limit of $5000 for bonds held by TreasuryDirect in electronic form.

Income - money you receive from various sources, such as employment, savings, investments, gifts, royalties, and retirement accounts.

Index - a statistical measurement of the performance of a group of data; e.g., financial securities such as stocks, bonds, or commodities; also a pointer on a scale to indicate value. In financial terms, an index is used to establish a relative value of a group of securities, usually on a daily basis.

Index fund - a fund composed of securities based upon a group, an index, of securities. These funds may be composed of stocks, bonds, or commodities. Index funds do not evaluate the potential for the underlying securities, but seek to match the security composition of the index.

Indexed CDs – a certificate of deposit linked to a financial index. The return is based on the performance of the index with limitations. Various limitations can be imposed which will limit the upside potential. If the index declines and the CD is held until maturity, the CD investor will get back the original investment.

Individual Retirement Account, Individual Retirement Arrangement (IRA), traditional - a retirement account set up by an individual with a financial institution acting as custodian of the funds and investments. The earnings and gains in the account are not taxed until funds are withdrawn. There are limits on the amount of annual contribution to the IRA and whether or not the contributions are tax deductible. Check the IRS web site, www.irs.gov/retirement, for the latest contribution limits. Also, see Roth IRA.

Intermediate-Term – a measurement of maturity for a fixed-income investment of one to ten years.

Joint tenancy (JT) - ownership of property/financial asset by two or more people. Your portion of the asset is passed on to your heirs or estate.

Joint tenancy with right of survivorship (JTWROS) - ownership of property/financial asset by two or more people. Upon your death, the other owners inherit your share of the asset.

Junk Bonds – bonds where the credit quality of the issuer is less than investment grade. These are high risk bonds with a questionable ability of the issuer to redeem the bond at maturity.

Ladder - see Bond Ladder or CD Ladder.

Lehman Aggregate Bond Index - an index of US government agency and corporate bonds. Reflects the US bond market. It is now called Barclays Capital Aggregate Bond Index.

Leverage - borrowing money to purchase an asset. Provides the ability to control or use an asset without putting up the full purchase price. This is commonly used by businesses to finance growth. Individuals also use leverage when borrowing money to purchase a home or vehicle. This *adds risk* to the company or individual depending upon the ratio of debt to the market value of the asset. If cash flow (disposable income) drops, and it becomes impossible to continue to make the loan payment, the asset may be sold, or repossessed, to pay off the debt. The difference between the sale price of the asset and the loan balance is the equity (ownership value) left in the asset. Leveraging works in an environment where the market value of the asset is increasing. When the market value of the asset declines, leverage can be disastrous, as exemplified in the housing market from 2007.

Liability - an obligation. In financial terms this is a debt, a loan, a promise to pay. Examples of a liability are your home mortgage, credit card debt, or vehicle loan.

Long-term – a measurement of maturity for a fixed-income investment of greater than 10 years.

Market Capitalization, Market-Cap - a measurement of a company based on its current market value. Calculated by multiplying the value of one share of stock by the number of shares of stock that are outstanding. In the United States, market-caps are currently defined as: Large-cap (over $10 billion), Mid-cap ($2-10 billion), Small-cap (under $2 billion).

Market-Cap index - a measurement of value of a group of stocks which are included in the group based on the size of their market capitalization. Such as large-cap, mid-cap, or small-cap stock index.

Maturity Date – the date on which a debt instrument – bond, certificate of deposit, loan – comes due. The principal amount (original investment) and any unpaid interest is paid to the holder (owner) of the debt instrument.

MSCI EAFE® - Morgan Stanley Capital International, Europe Australasia & Far East index; composed of 21 global stock market indices; a global stock index.

Mutual Fund - an investment fund (a company) which owns financial securities (stocks or bonds). The fund is run by an investment management firm. Shares of the fund are sold to individual investors at the daily calculated price: total market value of all the assets divided by the number of shares outstanding. The advantages offered by mutual funds are diversification, equal treatment of all investors regardless of amount invested, and professional management and selection of the investments. Beware, not all mutual funds live up to their advertised benefits. See Chapter 8.

Net discretionary income - as used in this book, is defined as gross income minus taxes and all items of spending. It is the amount of money you have left over for saving and investing. Also, see discretionary income.

Net worth - what you are worth financially. It is calculated as the total of all of your assets less all of your debts (liabilities). (Assets - Debts = Net Worth)

Non-Qualified Plan - an account that is subject to income tax during the year the account had earnings (interest, dividends, or capital gains). The account is *not-qualified* for tax-deferral.

Principal – the amount invested in a financial security, such as a bond or certificate of deposit.

Qualified Plan - an account which the IRS defines as meeting "the standards set forth in the Internal Revenue Code for tax-favored status." Tax-favored status means the plan *qualifies for tax deferral*. The earnings and capital gains in the account are not taxed until they are withdrawn.

Rebalancing – the process of redistributing financial assets among asset classes to maintain a desired asset mix. See Chapter 14, Maintaining Your Investment Plan.

Recession - a contraction in the economic activity of the country; a decline in employment, retail sales, and industrial output for two consecutive quarters, as measured by the Gross Domestic Product. Usually, the stock market will turn down a few months prior to the start of a recession and begin a recovery 6 months or more before the end of the recession.

Risk – the potential for loss in the value of an investment. Risk is linked to return or reward. The greater the potential for return on the investment, the greater the potential risk for loss of principal. See Chapter 6, Discover Your Risk Tolerance and Temperament.

Risk Tolerance – a measure of an investor's comfort level with investment volatility. See Chapter 6, Discover Your Risk Tolerance and Temperament.

Rollover - transferring of retirement monies from one retirement account or plan into another retirement account; e.g., the transfer of money from a 401(k) plan directly into a self-directed IRA. The transfer should take place between the old plan custodian and the new custodian without the owner receiving the funds. If the owner receives and holds the money, the IRS will impose taxes on the funds as if it were a distribution.

CD rollover - at maturity the accumulated value of a CD is automatically renewed; it is rolled over into a new CD of like duration, at the current interest rate.

Roth IRA - an individual retirement account similar to a traditional

IRA set up by an individual with a financial institution acting as custodian of the funds and investments. Unlike the traditional IRA, the earnings and appreciation of a Roth IRA are tax-free at withdrawal when certain restrictions are met. There are income and retirement plan participation limitations which may restrict or prevent contributions to a Roth IRA. Check the IRS web site, www.irs.gov/retirement, for the latest contribution limits. See IRA traditional.

Rule 72(t) - IRS rule that allows you to take withdrawals from your IRA before you reach 59½. The IRS permits you to take "a series of substantially equal payments over your life (or your life expectancy), or over the lives (or the joint life expectancies) of you and your beneficiary, without having to pay the 10% additional tax, even if you receive such distributions before you are age 59½."
(For more information, see IRS: www.irs.gov/publications/p590/ch01.html#en_US_publink10006428).

Russell 2000® - an index which measures the smaller 2000 companies of the Russell 3000® stock index based on market capitalization; a small Cap stock index.

S&P 500® - Standard & Poor 500®; an index measuring the performance of the 500 largest companies in the US, based on market capitalization; a Large Cap stock index.

Short-Term – a measurement of maturity for an investment of less than one year. This is used in reference to some fixed income investments and cash equivalents.

Simplified Employee Pension Plan (SEP-IRA) - a retirement plan in which an employer makes contributions into an employee's IRA. The IRA is owned by the employee.

TALF - Term Asset-Backed Securities Loan Facility - a program of the Federal Reserve in late 2008, to finance loans to consumers and small businesses for credit card loans, student loans, auto loans, and other such loans. This program was initially met with skepticism from financial institutions fearing unknown strings and consequences. The goal was to make credit available for consumers and small businesses.

Target-Date Funds - these funds portfolios own other mutual funds - a mix of equity and fixed income funds. These funds set target dates from a few years out to over 30 years into the future, usually in 5-year increments. As the target date approaches, the fund will become more conservative in its asset allocation, reducing the equity fund exposure and adding to fixed income. A typical target-date fund may have a targeted date in its name, such as Acme Target-Date 2030 Fund. *Not all target-date funds of the same duration or date use the same asset allocations. Investors should examine a funds allocation of equity and fixed income to determine if the fund matches their desired allocation.* In the 2008 market crash, target-date funds did not shield investors from loss. Some long-term funds experienced losses of over 40%, which was more than the decline of the S&P 500 index.

TARP - Troubled Asset Relief Program - developed in 2008 by the Federal government to allow the US Treasury to purchase up to $700 million of mortgages and mortgage-backed securities from financial institutions to promote the stability of the financial markets. The market for these mortgage-backed securities had dried up, and banks were not able to determine the value of the securities. The banks were then forced by the mark-to-market accounting rules to price these securities at greatly reduced values which negatively impacted their balance sheets, caused them to reduce lending activities and horde their cash to improve their balance sheet asset ratio. A goal of TARP was to get credit flowing again and stabilize the financial markets.

Tax-deferred - taxes are postponed (deferred) to a future time. Earnings on tax-deferred investments are not taxed in the year they are earned. Examples are IRAs, 401(k)s, and annuities. Don't confuse tax-deferred with tax-free.

Tax efficiency - refers to the tax consequences of mutual funds or ETFs from the investor's perspective. Tax efficient funds are managed to minimize the taxes paid by the fund or passed along to the investor. Taxes are due on trading profits of the fund and capital gains passed on to the investor.

Tax-free - earnings are not taxable, now or in the future. There are no federal income taxes on tax-free investments. Examples are interest on municipal bonds and earnings in Roth IRAs. However, your state may impose state income taxes on tax-free bonds and investments outside your state. The alternative minimum tax on income for federal tax calculations may also apply.

TIPS - Treasury Inflation-Protected Securities - US Government Bonds whose principal value adjusts to compensate for inflation or deflation.

- U.S. Government Treasury bond.
- Principal adjusts each year to reflect changes in consumer price index. This adjustment will reflect inflation or deflation.
- When held to maturity, you receive either the adjusted principal or the original principal, whichever is greater.
- Interest is paid out every six months at a fixed rate and is calculated on the new adjusted principal.
- Issued in 5-, 10-, or 20-year maturities.

These bonds are best used in a tax-deferred account, such as an IRA, in order to avoid capital gains taxes on an increase in the principal adjustment credited each year.

For additional information go to www.treasurydirect.gov/indiv/products/products.htm and choose TIPS from the left hand column. Also, see I-Bonds.

Treasuries - an expression that refers to US Government bonds, notes, and bills.

Vested - earned ownership. An employee owns the assets in an employer-sponsored retirement plan after certain conditions have been met, such as length of service. Vesting is irrevocable.

Wilshire 5000® - Dow Jones Wilshire 5000® index - an index of all publically traded stocks in the US. The index is composed of more than 6500 stocks.

Endnotes

Chapter 1

1. http://www.ssa.gov/finance/2006/FY06_PAR.pdf.
2. Martin Crutsinger, AP Economics Writer, Associated Press, "Social Security and Medicare Finances Worsen," May 12, 2009.
3. http://www.bea.gov/bea/newsrelarchive/2007/pi1206.pdf.
4. ftp.bls.gov/pub/special.requests/cpi/cpiai.txt .
5. *Retirement Information For Medicare Beneficiaries*, Social Security Admin., Publication No. 05-10529.

Chapter 2

6. Juanita Cousins. "Many states' lottery sales are rising in recession." Associated Press Archive. January 12, 2009.
7. http://www.nasd.com/PressRoom/NewsReleases/2006NewsReleases/NASDW_017386.
8. Stephen Greenspan, "Why We Keep Falling for Financial Scams," *The Wall Street Journal*, January 3, 2009.
9. *The Wall Street Journal*, "Investors' Lament: Buy High, Sell Low," May 18, 2009, P. C1.

Chapter 6

10. Amanda Gengler, Donna Rosato, Penelope Wang, "Survive the Worst-Case Scenario," *Money*, May, 2009, P. 99.

Chapter 7

11. http://www.finra.org/web/groups/Investors/@inv/@tools/documents/Investors/P014495.pdf.
12. http://www.finra.org/Investors/SmartInvesting/Retirement/p038342.
13. http://apps.finra.org/investor_Information/smart/bonds/106100.asp.

Chapter 8

14. Scott Burns, *Dallas Morning News*, May 14, 2009.
15. Eleanor Laise, "More Index Funds Sought for 401(k)s." *The Wall Street Journal, Money & Investing* section, July 18, 2009.
16. *Standard & Poor's Indices Versus Active Funds Scorecard, Year End 2008*, Standard & Poor's.

Chapter 11

17. www.sec.gov/news/press/2009/2009-32.htm.
18. *New York Times*, February 18, 2009.

Chapter 12

19. Internal Revenue Service, Publication 590, http://www.irs.gov/publications/p590.

Chapter 16

20. http://www.ssa.gov/retire2/fedgovees.htm.
21. http://www.ssa.gov/retire2/stateandlocal.htm.
22. http://www.socialsecurity.gov/retire2/agereduction.htm.

23. http://www.bls.gov/ces/.
24. http://www.socialsecurity.gov/retire2/whileworking.htm.

Chapter 19

25. http://www.socialsecurity.gov/OACT/COLA/latestCOLA.html.

Chapter 20

26. *The Wall Street Journal*, February 7, 2009, page B1.
27. *The Wall Street Journal*, March 17, 2009, page D1.
28. Kevin G. Hall, "Next taxpayer bailout: Life insurance companies." McClatchy Newspapers, April 8, 2009.
29. Janet Paskin, "More Insurers Raise Fee on Variable Annuities," *Smartmoney.com*, December 16, 2008.
30. Kimberly Lankford, "Variable Annuities with Guarantees Lose Appeal," *Kiplinger.com*, May 18, 2009.

www.ingramcontent.com/pod-product-compliance
Lightning Source LLC
Chambersburg PA
CBHW071355170526
45165CB00001B/50

* 9 7 8 1 4 6 0 9 6 6 9 8 3 *